Baby Names

How to Choose the Perfect Name for Your Baby

Including Thousands of Names with Meaning and Origin

Contents

PART 3: GLOSSARY OF NAMES

Introduction

Congratulations on the growth of your family! Whether this is your first baby or your tenth, your life is now full of little expectations and excitements. The number of people you love and who love you has been increased, and that is a thought worthy of celebration.

The presence of this little baby has no doubt been felt by the clothes, crib, stroller, car seat, and everything else you have been selecting. Everything you are buying is for your son or daughter. You're not the only person stockpiling for the wee one either. You are getting gifts you would like and maybe advice you wouldn't like. It may feel as if you are surrounding yourself with items that are for your child, as well as being squeezed out of situations and moments in place of the baby.

Parenting will be like that for years, perhaps even decades: moments that don't entirely belong to you or opportunities that you hand over for the sake of your children. Take heart, though, because there is one thing that belongs distinctly to you and your child alone…

The *name* of your baby.

This name will be a piece of yourself that your child will carry throughout their life, a reminder to the world that you have considered all possibilities and selected the best for your child. And because there is no right and wrong in personal taste, naming your child *anything* is your first success as a parent.

That being said, naming a child can be a bit daunting. It is a decision that lasts forever, and yet there is no way of knowing where that life will end up. Will your chosen name fit the occupation your child chooses or the personality they develop?

We are here to help answer those questions. This book will help you consider many factors in the naming process as well as provide categories of names and a glossary containing thousands of names with their meanings and origins. These names have been selected for their staying power, trendiness, or personalities. The lists are made up of names with certain ethnicities, histories, or considerations, such as powerful names and natural names.

The book is divided into three parts: how to choose a name that you enjoy and appreciate; lists of different names that you can use as inspiration; and a glossary of names so that you can see the variations and meanings behind the names you love.

We hope you enjoy the process. This is a monumental and exciting opportunity, and you shouldn't forget to enjoy it. Perhaps you will struggle through the process of naming your baby, perhaps you already have some names for consideration, and perhaps you have already selected your name. This book is for everyone. It will help you narrow your focus, and determine how you want the name of your baby to be used and enjoyed. Most of all, it will help you select one of the most lasting gifts you could ever give your baby, one thing that will outlast the cute outfits and trendy cribs…

The gift of identity.

Part 1: How to Choose a Name for Your Baby

In ancient Jewish culture, a name was much more than what you called your child; a name encapsulated personality, beliefs, and future destinies. Jewish parents would often consider what they wanted their children to be when selecting a name – name them "shepherd" if they will be a shepherd, or "sparkling beauty" if they are destined for beauty, or "wanderer" if they will be world travelers. Some also named their child for their personality, holding back on choosing a name sometimes for months until the baby's personality became apparent. To invoke someone's name was to invoke their entire being and existence.

The Puritans, who settled the American colonies, chose children's names out of their beliefs. Immigrants passing through Ellis Island either preserved their heritage in their names or found a way to Americanize them, symbolizing the new people they were becoming apart from their homeland. Slave owners in the American South changed their slaves' names when they arrived from Africa. There is nothing more demoralizing and ostracizing than committing an identity to death. In turn, slaves would secretly name their children the old African names they once possessed.

Comparably, concentration camps during World War II would assign numbers to people instead of their titles. Names have an uncanny ability to adapt to people and create or relinquish identity and personhood.

When we remember people individually or as a society, we remember their attributes or actions. But we assign those qualities to a name. The appellation Martin Luther King Jr. evokes a memory of words, doings, successes, and tragedies all brought about by one person. We remember in names. A name, therefore, has weight beyond the life of one individual. The tradition of naming sons after fathers (juniors, the seconds, the thirds, so on) and changing last names in the same ilk (Andrew's son will be called by the surname "Anderson") has adopted this idea of transference of memory.

The point of this information is not to bog you down by making sure your name is 'perfect'; otherwise, history will never forgive you. It is to show how the designations you use for your little ones will forever represent the relationship between you and them. It is your declaration to the rest of the world, to history, of the love you have for your baby, and that the relationship between you has been determined prior to all other relationships.

This is a high honor, but it is also a sweet and secret moment that no one else will replicate with your child. You, your partner, and your baby will always share the bond of that name, no matter where the circumstances of life take any of you.

Now, with this love and moment in mind, let's take a look at how you can choose a name that you will enjoy and appreciate for all time.

Where to Start

It may seem as if the beginning portion of choosing a name is the hardest part, but the fact that there are thousands of possibilities gives you a wide starting platform. You can consider so many things when you are starting the naming process, and that allows you to dream large and consider many options.

The following sections will help you consider where to begin when selecting a name.

Gender

Gender will probably be the most significant consideration when naming your child. There are distinctions between names that have been socially accepted and utilized for boys and girls, but selecting for gender need not stop there. Beyond deciding on a gender-determined name for your baby once you know the gender (or when you will know the gender), you can also decide if you will choose a name despite gender.

It has become popular in modern society to choose boys' names for girls (i.e., James, Ryan) or even feminine spellings or nicknames of male names for girls (Charley for Charlotte, George for Georgina). You can choose more feminine renderings for boys (Jayden, Blayke) or girls' names themselves (Cat, Jessi) for your baby boy. You can also decide to use an androgynous name, like Andy or Peyton, to cross between the genders.

Gender is the starting point for choosing a name for your baby, but it is not about deciding between two genders. Feel free to pick a male name for boys or girls, a female name for boys or girls, or a name that has been used for both boys and girls. You select your name in response to gender. Start from there, and then consider if the next step is important to you.

Lineage

Depending on your upbringing or heritage, lineage may play a big part in naming your child. Lineage, however, can have multiple connotations and multiple choices within that broad consideration.

If you hail from a specific ethnicity, you may choose to name your baby something within that ethnicity. For example, if your Irish heritage is important to you and/or your partner, you may want to consider naming your baby something with Irish history. This may be the only part of the process of naming your baby that includes other people – where your family claims their history could influence how your baby claims that same history as well.

Lineage, though, could also represent people in your past. Most commonly, baby boys could be named for their father in the use of a junior title or adding "second" or "third" to that name. It is not as common for daughters and mothers, but it is a possibility. Maybe you are wishing to honor your great-grandmother by including her name as your baby girl's middle name or using a hybrid of her name as a new name. Your lovely grandmother, Anne, and strong great-aunt, Marie, could become your lovely and strong daughter, Annamarie. Heritage of name is another way memories carry themselves.

A place can have its own remembrances. A couple who honeymooned in France may be attracted to the name Paris. If New York City holds a special place in your heart because you were raised there, Brooklyn or Bronx would be a precious homage to those moments. The important thing about lineage is the memory, and there are many ways to capture a memory.

There is another avenue to lineage, too, which is the heritage of someone not related to you, but important to you. A social activist, a famous poet, a celebrity, the seventh-grade math teacher who believed in you, all may hold certain traits that you would like to see passed on to your child. Even fictional characters have their hold on baby-naming trends. The generations who grew up believing in the magic of the *Harry Potter* saga are more likely to name their daughters Hermione. The rise of Aaron Rodgers saw the rise of the name Aaron. People are influential, and their names are influential. Naming your baby after someone important to you is one way to carry on their legacy for the next generation.

Beliefs

Just like lineage, beliefs cover multiple avenues of naming opportunities. This most commonly means your religious beliefs, though a lack of religious beliefs could also have an impact on choosing a name. For example, the name Grace is more common in Christian circles for its connection to God's grace, but the name could also mean grace of poise and elegance and may be used by people with no religious affiliation. Muhammad is the most common name on the planet at the time of this writing, yet it has a strong heritage that may impress beyond its religious connotation.

You may also consider less explicit references to beliefs. If protecting the seas from pollution is your passion, names like Purity and Ocean may find themselves as contenders in your book. Practicers of yoga, regardless of spiritual connection, may like the haunting sound of the name Ohm.

Beliefs have a way of finding their way into our naming choices. Whether your religious affiliation or personal drive play into how you name your baby, the barest form of beliefs can be how you choose your name and what that name may be. You believe in naming your baby the best name possible, and that belief is the one that will carry your process and ultimate destination.

Meaning

The meaning has connections with both lineage and beliefs, but it could also stand alone as a consideration when naming your baby. When we discuss meaning, however, we discuss the literal definition of a name. This does, though, encapsulate beliefs.

If the concept of light has importance to you according to your religious beliefs, you may consider searching for a name that means light, like Luz or Luke or Lucia. Meaning can build a future for your child as well. If you want your baby to grow up into a gentle being, you may pick a name that denotes gentleness. Meaning can be a vital part of choosing a name.

Sound

Another consideration is sound. This may seem like an odd purpose, but choosing a name due to its sound can have just as much impact as meaning.

To illustrate this principle, consider J.R.R. Tolkien's *The Lord of the Rings* trilogy. This may seem like a silly exercise, but consider how he used his choice of character names to illustrate the mentalities and attributes of them. His stronger characters had names that sounded strong: Boromir, Sauron, Saruman. Notice the use of the "r" sounds. Names with that same sound tend to have that same strength and punctuation you would expect in someone who would take charge, like Robert or Carter. On the other hand, when Tolkien was going for stateliness or gentleness over strength, he picked names with "l" and "n" sounds: Galadriel, Arwen.

This isn't a fictional rule; this is simple linguistics. Certain sounds carry certain connotations to the native English speaker. We find "sh" sounds comforting and attach a certain beauty and firmness in names like Shawn and Rashelle. "G" sounds have a stronger, harsher sound that causes us to pause; Graham and Geri make us stop and listen up because the sounds don't fall as gently in the English language.

You may also like the sound of some portions of a name. Simply eliminate the sounds you don't like, either by removing them entirely or replacing them with different sounds for a unique twist on a classic. Not a fan of the B in Bethany? Remove it to make Ethany, or replace it for Sethany. Name rules are fluid and available for restructuring. You just need to find something that works for you.

The pronunciation of vowels used could make a difference in the way a name is utilized and interpreted. For example, the name Roan (pronounced Rohn and rhyming with zone) has a softer sound to it than the more common name Ron because Roan has a short vowel rather than a long vowel. You can play with the sounds you like best; don't like the longer vowel sound at the front of Ava (pronounced Ayvuh)? Try exchanging it for the short vowel Ava (pronounced Ahvuh) without changing the spelling, or change the spelling to represent the sound change.

To be fair to the less-pleasing sounds within names, there is nothing wrong with them. Names with harsh consonants and long vowels don't have softer edges; they are strong and convincing and ready for the world. It all depends on how you want your child to be perceived based on their title. A Keely may have a stronger personality than a Kelly, but a Kelly may adopt that more gentle and steady nature than Keely.

Spelling

The final consideration that will help you pick the best baby name for you and your child is spelling. It has become popular in modern times to seek out different spellings for names. Kaylee, Aiden, and many other titles find themselves spelled multiple ways according to fashion or preference.

It will be up to you and your partner to consider the possible spellings out there for the names you like. We have provided alternative spellings in the glossary of names. You may be inclined to make up your own spelling.

Consider, too, how other people will pronounce the spelling of your child's name. Some spellings, based on their particular spelling and ethnicity, will always need clarification: children answering to Beau and Niamh may have to correct their teachers throughout their school years. However, an overcomplicated spelling of a more common name may result in confusion. It may be wise to see if your family members and friends can pronounce the names you have selected.

After all these points have been considered, you may have a good idea of which names are making the top ten within your selections. You may have found yourself eliminating some names, and that is perfectly fine! If, however, you find yourself with multiple names that you love equally, reading the next section may help you find a place for those lovely designations.

Picking Multiple Names

Though there is a list in the next part of the book that discusses cute and clever combinations for siblings, this multiple names section is not designed for that purpose. Instead, we will look at ways to incorporate your favorite names and create functional and pleasing first and middle name combinations.

First is combining names. Sometimes, you may like the sound and meaning of two names equally and are considering how to utilize both titles in your baby's name. It is common to combine names with girls, but there are ways to do the same with boys. Most names will follow a simple principle. You may find a combination of two names that makes you happier than one name by itself.

For any name, male or female, decide what kind of combination you would like. Would you prefer giving your child two names as a first name, or smashing two names together to create a new one? Either option is viable but will take some consideration.

To give your baby two first names, you will simply need to see how they sound in combination with your last name – and with a middle name if you have already selected one. The English-speaking ear prefers an even number of syllables for consistency, but that is not a hard and fast rule to picking baby names. Remember, you are the one who gets the final say. It may be a good starting place, however. An even number of syllables sounds comforting, an odd number of syllables sounds melodic.

For an example of a boy's name, let's consider the name Everett James. James for your father and Everett for your partner's father. That is three syllables already, and that's a great start. Now consider how Everett James will sound with your last name. Your last name is two syllables. You still have an odd number of syllables. You must decide to maintain consistency or go for a unique sound. A two-syllable middle name for the latter, a one-syllable name for the former. Everett James Scott Whiteman sounds lyrical, Everett James Rupert Whiteman sounds sturdy.

Do the following with girls' names. Anna Renee. Brittany Jean. You have endless possibilities in combining names, and you aren't obligated to select just one name. As a bonus, your baby can later choose which name to shorten as a nickname. Brittany Jean can become the adorable androgynous BJ.

Combining two names into one name may be delicate, but it is doable. The trick is to find a correct breaking point in the name. This usually comes at a syllable break. You can decide how much of each name to include in the combination. Let's take our boy's name, Everett James, and our girl's name, Brittany Jean, as examples.

The break in Everett could occur at the Ev- or Ever-, creating Evames or Everames. The break in Brittany comes at Br- or Britt-. Brean or Brittean. You may want to alter the spellings of the combinations for ease of pronunciation.

Multiple names also include consideration of middle names. Middle names are a bit looser in consequence than first names, as only the birth certificate gets a regular reminder of that second title. However, all professional and academic communication will utilize the middle name, so it is good to consider it. It's not uncommon to choose a tamer middle name if you are going for a bolder first name, but there is no rule to that. A Wolfe Thomas Anderson is not guaranteed a more successful life than a Wolfe Midnight Anderson. It is worth your consideration, though, to think about what would happen if your child prefers going by their middle name later in life. If he or she has a more unique first name, they may feel more comfortable going by a quieter middle name. Especially in those teenage years.

These ideas and pointers will help guide your decisions, but they need not be your only guides. Trust your taste. You alone – or you and your partner if relevant – have the best ideas for your names. If you like something or a certain name keeps grabbing your attention, go for it. Go for all of them. Have four or five names if you love them all. You are only giving your child more identities to choose from, more nicknames to select, and in a world that offers very little choices in fates, that may be a comforting thing to have.

The Tests of a Good Name

Now that you have got a few names rolling around, it is time for the ultimate tests of whether or not you are making the right choice. These tests are more contexts in which your child's name will be tossed into a trial, and your response to each name in each context may help you weed out some of the outliers.

You may need your partner or a friend for this first test: the Playground Test. It will be an amusing test, so recruit someone with an incredible sense of humor. Grab your favorite non-alcoholic beverage, hand your partner a glass of wine, and pretend you are yelling at your child on a playground. Practice a nice "don't stray too far" yell and a serious "you knock that off" yell. Is your favorite name easy to yell across a playground? Is it too long? Can it be taken seriously? This may be an activity that will repeat itself in your life, so make it a good one. See if your favorite names, though too long, can be shortened in a moment of crisis or sand-eating.

The second test is the President Test. Place the word "president" in front of your child's full name – if you have selected one. You may not have presidential hopes for your baby, but the point of the exercise is to see if the name you have selected can be taken seriously in a professional setting. If "president" sounds like too much pressure, try "lawyer" or "doctor". It is the same principle; will the names you have chosen operate well in a professional setting? This may be a subjective test, but perhaps your child may have dreams of being a doctor or a political activist in a professional setting, and a manageable name may help you determine the direction of your selections.

The third test is similar to the Playground Test. It's called the Announcer Test. Now the odds are good that your baby may not be the next NFL quarterback, but this test helps you check the flow of a first and last name combination. Pretend your child has just entered the field, ring, stage, platform of your choosing, and announce their name as if they are the main attraction. Say it with importance and magnitude. Does Caroline Avila mesh nicely? Does Ricky Thornton? Again, this is not so much as choosing the fame of your child, but considering how the two names will function in everyday society. After all, your baby will experience roughly twelve years of their first and last names being called together on a classroom roll call list.

The last test is the Relative Test. This does not mean that you ask each surviving relative what they think of the baby names you have chosen. Instead, run through the titles of relatives and see how your name fits into each position. If you think Grandpa Freddy is adorable, but Uncle Freddy feels too clunky, you may want to consider an alternative nickname or lengthening the name overall to find a fit you like. Go through Cousin Avery, Grandma Avery, Aunt Avery. Find a name that sounds comfortable to you in every context.

A Final Thought on Picking the Perfect Name

There is no perfect name. At least, not in a universal sense. The perfect name is a name that is perfect for you, your partner, and your baby. The perfect name is the name that perfectly encapsulates the love that you have for one another. Beyond all other considerations, that is the point that matters most.

There is no Nickname Test as cruelty can find a way to make a nickname out of even the most innocent moniker. There is no Connotation Test because every name will remind someone of someone else and what they symbolize. You will not win over the entire world with your name. There will be people who despise your simple name for its simplicity and people who hate your unique name for its uniqueness.

However, it is not your job to please everybody. It is your job to give your baby the best name you can imagine in the moments you have to select a name. Don't worry about finding the name that perfectly describes your child's hopes, personality, and future. No one can know how each child will turn out. The best you can do is raise your baby well, and that begins by putting honest thought into picking a name. If that honest thought is poring over every name book in existence, then that is your honest thought. If your honest thought is remembering a boy in high school with that cool name you have always liked, that is your honest thought. There is no judgment in taste, and there is no right or wrong way to pick a name that accurately portrays the relationship you have with your child.

Your little baby already has a personhood, but his or her name will grant them the first marks of personal identity. Of all the gifts of toys and clothing and furniture you can give your little one, the gift of identity will be the foundation upon which the rest of their lives are built. Take a moment to not stress or worry that you won't do a good job, but appreciate that knowledge for the precious bond you and your partner share with your baby.

Moreover, above all things, enjoy the process of naming your baby. It is a once-in-a-lifetime opportunity, and in this moment, you are not only creating a life but a living identity.

Part 2: Categorized Lists of Names

You may have some ideas about how you plan to choose a name for your child, or maybe you even have a few names selected. Maybe you are feeling overwhelmed with the thought of handling someone's moniker for the rest of their life. Regardless of where you stand, it may be helpful to see some lists of names that have been divided into different categories of interest.

We have rounded up various categories of names to help you narrow down your search. These names have been divided by popularity, rising fashion, ethnicities, and even types of names, such as natural or powerful choices. There are many more names than just the ones provided, but it may be useful to see where your names of choice would be placed. It may also be helpful to consider what you would like your name to offer. Should it be a name that has stood the test of time? Should it be a name that evokes a specific time or place? Questions such as these can guide your decisions.

Each list contains an explanation of why these names were chosen within the category. The names within each list are alphabetized for your convenience. Though the origins and meanings of names are not given here, the glossary of names following this section will provide such.

When practical, the names have been divided by the genders. We have included a list of names that have remained popular for both boys and girls. There is even a list of names that could be combined for siblings.

Enjoy your reading, and we hope that these lists will confirm your choices or open a new realm of possibilities for your name selections.

Boy Names with Staying Power

These are names that have remained popular with male children throughout the last one hundred years (roughly 1915 to present), according to the United States Social Security Administration. These names are not alphabetized but listed numerically in order of popularity over the last century.

1. James (Jamie, Jim, Jimmy)
2. John (Jon, Johnny, Jonny)
3. Robert (Rob, Bob, Bobby)
4. Michael (Mike, Mikael)
5. William (Will, Bill, Billy)
6. David (Dave)
7. Richard (Rick, Rich)
8. Joseph (Joe, Josef)
9. Thomas (Tom, Tommy, Tomas)
10. Charles (Charley, Charlie, Chuck)

Girl Names with Staying Power

These are names that have remained popular with female children throughout the last one hundred years (roughly 1915 to present), according to the United States Social Security Administration. These names are not alphabetized but listed numerically in order of popularity over the last century.

1. Mary (Marie)
2. Patricia (Tricia, Patty)
3. Jennifer (Jen, Jenny)
4. Linda
5. Elizabeth (Beth, Liz, Lizzy, Eliza)
6. Barbara
7. Susan
8. Jessica (Jess, Jessie, Jesse)
9. Sarah/Sara
10. Margaret (Maggie, Marge)

Androgynous Names

These are names that could be used for boys or girls. In fact, many of these names have become just as popular with one gender as they have with the other. Other names on this list may have started out in favor with one gender, and now are becoming more popular with the other gender. Different spellings are offered where ideal.

Addison	Harper
Andy/Andi/Andee	Harlow
Bennett	Jaden
Berkeley	Jamie
Bowen	Lane
Casey	Lark
Coby/Cobie	Mackenzie
Colby	Micah
Court	Parker
Danny/Dani	Peyton
Devon	Quinn
Elliot	

Sibling Combinations for Boys and Girls

These names are in combinations of two and three for children with multiple births in the family, or if you are thinking down the line for other children. They are not alphabetized and not specifically divided into genders. They were selected for their similar sounds.

Jack and Dax	Aiden and Brayden

Arlo and Milo

Nathaniel and Natalie

Madison and Miranda

Susanna, Shawna, and Sophia

Callie and Allie

Parker, Paige, and Paris

Cora and Court

Preston, Nelson, and Weston

Andrea and Andrew

Eric, Derek, and Alec

Titus and Tatiana

Natural Names for Boys and Girls

These names are related to natural elements. They are not divided into gender.

	Fisher	Oak
Bear	Forrest	Opal
Cale	Fox	River
Crystal	Heather	Ruby
Dahlia	Iris	Savannah
Dawn	Ivy	Sierra
Fawn	Lake	Violet
Fern	Lily	Willow

Location Names for Boys and Girls

These are names inspired by different places around the world. They are not divided into genders as most of them are androgynous. The places of inspiration have been specified.

Brooklyn

Named for a borough of New York City, Brooklyn is a popular name for girls.

Cairo

For Cairo, the metropolitan capital of Egypt, and the home of the Giza pyramids. Boys and girls alike can benefit from this exotic moniker.

Dax

A commune in Landes, France, which specializes in relaxation resorts and spas.

Devon

Devonshire, a county in England, is known for its brilliant green meadows. This name evokes natural beauty.

Houston

For Houston, the most populous city in Texas. Houston is fast becoming a global cuisine mecca, and your little one's name will reflect that worldliness.

Montgomery

The culinary capital of Alabama and the center for the Civil Rights Movement of the mid-twentieth century. This town name celebrates its past and present, and your child's historical connection embraces Montgomery's future.

London

For London, England. London is home to a melting pot of royalty, regality, and rock and roll. From princesses to punk fashion, a boy or girl named London reflects the cultural unities seen in England's capital.

Orlando

Orlando, Florida, is home to more than a dozen theme parks. Though more popular with boys, girls will appreciate this fun-loving, sunny state name.

Paris

Paris, France, has a romantic connotation that will never shake. Boys and girls named from the city of light and love have a romantic atmosphere.

Taos

A unique choice for either gender, Taos, New Mexico, is known for its art scene, ski resorts, and healing centers. This name elicits ideas of ancient civilizations and modern spirituality.

Tennessee

Whether you're choosing Tennessee for its rural beauty, artistic appreciation, or musical history, this sweet and strong name appeals to both genders. Consider a nickname like Tenn or Ness if the length concerns you.

Irish Names for Boys

These names are selected from Part 3: Glossary of Names for their Irish heritage for baby boys. Alternative spellings and meanings are not listed but will be listed in the glossary.

Bain	Grady	Niall
Casey	Houston	Orin
Cillian	Keagan	Quillen
Darin	Lachlan	Rory
Declan	Mackenzie	Troy
Donovan	Murphey	

Irish Names for Girls

These names are selected from Part 3: Glossary of Names for their Irish heritage for baby girls. Alternative spellings and meanings are not listed but will be listed in the glossary.

Bria	Fiona	Keira
Darcy	Imogene	Kelly

Kylie	Niamh	Shawna
Lana	Peyton	Siobhan
Molly	Quinn	Tawny

French Names for Boys

These names are selected from Part 3: Glossary of Names for their French heritage for baby boys. Alternative spellings and meanings are not listed but will be listed in the glossary.

Beau	Gage	Orville
Blais	Gilbert	Porter
Cabe	Jacques	Tiesen
Dax	Marshall	Vern
Forrest	Montgomery	Yvo

French Names for Girls

These names are selected from Part 3: Glossary of Names for their French heritage for baby girls. Alternative spellings and meanings are not listed but will be listed in the glossary.

Alina	Jacqueline	Raina
Collette	Jewel	Renee
Demi	Joanna	Ryann
Destiny	Julie	Scarlett
Evelyn	Lacy	Yvette
Fawn	Macy	
Genevieve	Noel	

German Names for Boys

These names are selected from Part 3: Glossary of Names for their German heritage for baby boys. Alternative spellings and meanings are not listed but will be listed in the glossary.

Armando	Geoffrey	Norman
Bruno	Harrison	Oberon
Charles	Henry	Otis
Derek	March	Rab
Fitzgerald	Liam	Reinhart

Schaeffer	Varrick	Walter

German Names for Girls

These names are selected from Part 3: Glossary of Names for their German heritage for baby girls. Alternative spellings and meanings are not listed but will be listed in the glossary.

Ada	Giselle	Louise
Adaline	Greta	Marley
Alicia	Harriet	Robin
Bernadette	Heidi	Rosamund
Carolina	Ilse	Rosalind
Ella	Jocelyn	Tilly

Powerful Names for Boys

These names were chosen for their strength. Boys with these names can expect to carry a legacy of power and respect. Alternative spellings and meanings are not listed but will be listed in the glossary.

Archer	Ilan	Wright
Brandt	Mariner	Wyeth
Clark	Marius	Xander
Court	Rab	
Hall	Sol	

Powerful Names for Girls

These names were chosen for their strength. Girls with these names can expect to carry a legacy of power and respect. Alternative spellings and meanings are not listed but will be listed in the glossary.

Ariel	Etta	Nova
Athena	Fortuna	Octavia
Bernice	Grier	Petra
Devon	Justine	Zara
Edith	Lara	

Simple and Sweet Names for Boys

As opposed to their bold-sounding counterparts, these names were chosen for their appeal and simplicity. The sound of these names are pleasing and evoke a sense of quiet dignity and gentleness for your baby boy. Alternative spellings and meanings are not listed but will be listed in the glossary.

Blane	Griff	Owen
Cisco	Hugo	Sol
Colby	Mac	Wade
Elias	Mateo	

Simple and Sweet Names for Girls

As opposed to their bold-sounding counterparts, these names were chosen for their appeal and simplicity. The sound of these names are pleasing and evoke a sense of quiet dignity and gentleness for your baby girl. Alternative spellings and meanings are not listed but will be listed in the glossary.

Amelia	Eloise	Macy
Arely	Heather	Nora
Charlotte	Kara	Patrice
Daisy	Lana	Quinn
Damaris	Libby	Saida

Last Names as First Names for Boys and Girls

These names became popular for surnames, but are now climbing the ranks as first names. They are not divided into genders as most of them are androgynous. Alternative spellings and meanings are not listed but will be listed in the glossary.

Anderson	Griffin	Nelson
Bennett	Holden	Parker
Cooper	Jefferson	Porter
Davis	Lincoln	Webster
Emerson	Mackenzie	

Literature-Inspired Names for Boys

These names tell a story. They were taken from stories of classic and modern literature. Each name has a literary-inspired connection, and people meeting your little boy will be charmed by the connotation he carries. Each name has an explanation of its origin in literature, though alternative spellings and meanings will only be listed in the following glossary.

Alcott

Though inspired by Louisa May Alcott, author of 'Little Women', your little boy will still appreciate the familial devotion and comfort that this name evokes.

Atticus

Named for the steady father and lawyer in Harper Lee's 'To Kill a Mockingbird', your son's wisdom and compassion will serve him well.

Barrett

Poet Elizabeth Barrett Browning is the namesake for your boy, but he will benefit from her beautiful poetry and devotion to her husband, Robert Browning.

Conrad

Joseph Conrad wrote the Modernist novella, 'Heart of Darkness', but there is nothing dark about this name. Conrad's shrewd discernment of mankind made for a moving tale of desire and power, and such a compelling story will make for a compelling boy.

Cowper

William Cowper (pronounced Cooper) was an English poet who changed the way people thought of nature through his beautiful writing. This name sounds strong but has a softer, natural side.

Dartagnan

D'Artagnan was the youthful addition to the Three Musketeers in Dumas' novel.

Spunky and exotic, this name can be shortened to the modern moniker Dart.

Heathcliff

No name invokes images of wild moors, craggy castles, deep bloodlines, and profound love than Heathcliff, the protagonist of Emily Bronte's 'Wuthering Heights'. Go for the nickname Heath to modernize it, but keep the longer version as inspiration for dark nights and passionate romance.

Ishmael

Most people haven't read 'Moby-Dick', but most people know the novel's opening line: "Call me Ishmael." Your son will get a few chuckles when he introduces himself as such. This name is antiquated but has the softer sounds and masculine charm of a modern name.

Marlowe

An alternative spelling of Marlow, Marlowe is the hero of Conrad's 'Heart of Darkness'. He travels deep into Africa to condemn the horrors of power gone astray. A boy with this name can adopt the same world-wanderer spirit that champions justice.

Ulysses

Ulysses is the hero of Homer's 'The Odyssey', a mighty warrior who works hard to get his men home safely. Both presidential and heroic, there is no losing with this name.

Virgil

Virgil was a poet in Ancient Greece, writing the mighty epic, 'The Aeneid'. He later appears in Dante's 'Inferno' to guide Dante and inspire him. Whether you prefer the muse or the master poet, Virgil is a name with an otherworldly appeal.

Walden

Walden was not a person, but a place. Named for Henry David Thoreau's individualistic encounters with nature, this soft-sounding name contains centuries of poetry, nature, and self-sufficiency.

Zane

A more modern literature-inspired name, Zane is for Zaen Grey, an American Western writer. The name still holds the same rugged appeal.

Literature-Inspired Names for Girls

These names tell a story. They were taken from stories of classic and modern literature. Each name has a literary-inspired connection, and people meeting your little girl will be charmed by the connotation she carries. Each name has an explanation of its origin in literature, though alternative spellings and meanings will only be listed in the following glossary.

Annabel

Named for Edgar Allen Poe's beautiful and haunting poem about the death of his precious Annabel Lee, this classic and charming name will be perfect for a baby girl so memorable people will write poems about her.

Beatrice

Beatrice can be shortened to Bea or Trice, but there is nothing tiny about the namesake. The heroine of Shakespeare's 'Much Ado About Nothing', Beatrice wins the heart of her stubborn lover with her own stubbornness, beauty, and wit.

Catherine

There are many Catherines in literature to choose from. Perhaps the most famous is Catherine from 'Wuthering Heights', the untamed beauty who refused to be separated from her lover, even in death. The same steadfastness, wildness, and beauty can be found in a girl with this classic name.

Charlotte

Charlotte is a lovely name with a daring namesake. Any baby girl would be proud to carry the name of Charlotte Bronte, who wrote an empowering book when no one believed a woman could do it.

Daphne

Daphne has a sweet sound, but Daphne du Maurier was a bold woman who wrote such chilling mysteries as 'Rebecca' and 'The Birds'. Famous for her horror and slow-burning books, the name Daphne carries a lovely mystique to it. A baby girl named Daphne will have a softer side, but she can also be a master of mystery.

Elizabeth

Who could forget Elizabeth Bennett, the plucky and thoughtful heroine of 'Pride and Prejudice'? Your daughter can keep the longer name or do as our heroine did and go by the even cuter nickname, Lizzy.

Fantine

With movies and musicals abounding, the tragic heroine of Fantine from 'Les Misérables' has become popular. She represents grace, forgiveness, and doing anything for her family. May your little girl carry the same beauty and determination as her namesake.

Jane

The heroine of 'Jane Eyre' is anything but plain, and your daughter will carry on the same tenacity and wit as she. Jane sticks to her convictions, matches those around her for strength and courage, and perseveres for love.

Jo/Josephine

You may call her Josephine, but Jo from 'Little Women' would never be called anything other than her fiery nickname. Her attachment to family and staying true to herself will be a great inspiration for your baby girl.

Portia

Though it sounds powerful, Portia is the name of the woman who gave the world its most famous speech on mercy. Your daughter will have the same courage, wisdom, and merciful spirit as Shakespeare's heroine from 'The Merchant of Venice'.

Ramona

Ramona Quimby has delighted readers for years, and the same spunky and good-hearted spirit can be found in a daughter named for her.

Scout

In Harper Lee's 'To Kill a Mockingbird', readers are treated to the determined, heartfelt narration of young Scout, Atticus Finch's precocious daughter. She is thoughtful, loving, and plucky, and your baby girl can carry the same attributes with this fun name.

Mythology-Inspired Names for Boys

These names are eternally linked to the gods of lore. Whether famous for strength, cunning, or attractiveness, your little boy's name will have the same attributes. Each name has an explanation of its origin, though alternative spellings and meanings will only be listed in the following glossary.

Achilles

A famous Greek warrior in Homer's the 'Iliad', Achilles was a demigod with strength and beauty. Your son will hold the same romantic appeal.

Adonis

Any little boy named Adonis has quite the legend to live up to; Adonis was the most handsome man on Earth. He was so attractive that he was the favorite lover of the goddess Aphrodite.

Ajax

Ajax is also from Homer's the 'Iliad'. He was known for his strength and determination. Your son will have the same qualities with this unique yet modern name.

Apollo

There is a certain poetic justice in naming your son for the god of the sun. If you think that's too energetic of a name for your boy, consider that Apollo was also the god of poetry and music.

Atlas

Your baby boy will have a strong personality when he is named for Atlas, the Titan who holds up the Earth in Greek mythology.

Odin

Odin is not a Greek god, but a Norse god who is the ruler of Earth. The name has a pleasing sound but contains a connotation of great power, which your little boy will appreciate.

Thor

Thor is also a Norse god, and the name is growing in popularity with the influence of pop culture. You can choose your inspiration from the storm god of legend or the witty companion of the movies for your son.

Mythology-Inspired Names for Girls

These names are eternally linked to the goddesses of lore. Whether famous for strength, cunning, or attractiveness, your little girl's name will have the same attributes. Each name has an explanation of its origin, though alternative spellings and meanings will only be listed in the following glossary.

Athena

A beautiful name for your baby girl, Athena will remind people of the goddess of justice, wisdom, courage, and strength. Could there be a more beautiful connotation?

Callie/Calliope

Calliope is not the most common of names, but it would be an excellent choice for parents who want a daughter gifted in the arts. Calliope is the name of the Greek muse who inspires eloquence and poetry. Consider the nickname Cal or Callie for your sweet speaker.

Diana

Diana was the goddess of the hunt, and your baby girl can have the same quickness of foot and mind that made Diana so strong and lovely. In a more modern interpretation, Diana evokes the attributes of Wonder Woman. Who wouldn't want her strength and heart of gold?

Freya

Freya is the Norse goddess who rules over all the other deities. She is the goddess of love and life, and her name evokes the same delicate grace that can be given to your little girl.

Boy Names in 2018

These are names for baby boys that are on the rise for 2018. These monikers have been growing in popularity over time and are now the most popular names in the United States. They are listed alphabetically, not in order of popularity, and meanings and origins are offered in the glossary.

Atticus

Carter

Grant

Jackson

Jasper

Lincoln

Logan

Milo

Pierce

Wade

Girl Names in 2018

These are names for baby girls that are on the rise for 2018. These monikers have been growing in popularity over time and are now the most popular names in the United States. They are listed alphabetically, not in order of popularity, and meanings and origins are offered in the glossary.

Alexia	Luna
Bridget	Madison
Eleanor	Margaret
Freya	Ruth
Harley	Saoirse
Iris	Sophia

Retro Boy Names

Everything old is new again, and these boy names are experiencing a revival. They are listed alphabetically; meanings and origins will be found in the glossary.

Amos	Hank
Booker	Hudson
Callum	Jasper
Edison	Marius
Emerson	Vincent
Franklin	

Retro Girl Names

Everything old is new again, and these girl names are experiencing a revival. They are listed alphabetically; meanings and origins will be found in the glossary.

Amelia	Gwen
Beatrice	Leonora
Darla	Pearl
Evelyn	Rosamund
Felicity	Winifred

Part 3: Glossary of Names

Now that you have considered which names would work best for you based on general selection principles and the different lists offered, it may be helpful to look through a glossary of names. This glossary contains the names mentioned in each list as well as over 1000 other options. Everything is alphabetically listed.

The names have been divided into names for baby boys and baby girls. However, you are naming your child. Your beliefs, lifestyle, and childrearing ideals make each child's name dependent upon your choices. If you prefer to name your daughter a masculine name, as is popular amongst celebrities today, you may. If you wish to name your son a name listed in the girls' section, you may. Select an androgynous name that would work for a boy or a girl.

To easier locate the name you are considering, all names are alphabetized within their gender groupings. We have also included alternative spellings or nicknames beneath each name so that you can see different options available to you. The list of alternative spellings is not exhaustive; utilize some creative license to determine which spelling appeals to you. Also included in each name is its language of origin – to the best of linguists' knowledge – and its meaning, if either option is to be taken into consideration.

At the end of the day, what you have before you is a guide. The lists themselves are not exhaustive. We have selected names that are common, some names that are on the rise, and some names that have stood the test of time.

There are so many possibilities out there, and we hope this glossary will help you have a better understanding of each name.

Boy Names

The names in this glossary have been predominantly used for boys throughout their use in history, though there is no rule that the same names can't be given to girls (for a collection of androgynous names, see the corresponding list). They are listed alphabetically and offer multiple spellings and possible shortenings and nicknames.

A

Aaron

Alternative uses: Aron, Arron, Aaryn

Origin: Hebrew

Meaning: mountain of strength

Abbot

Alternative uses: Abbott

Origin: British

Meaning: father or priest

Abdal

Alternative uses: Abdall

Origin: Arabic

Meaning: servant

Abdallah

Alternative uses: Abdallah

Origin: Arabic

Meaning: God's servant

Abel

Alternative uses: Abell, Abele

Origin: Hebrew

Meaning: breath, life

Abraham

Alternative uses: Abram, Abe

Origin: Hebrew

Meaning: father of a people or multitude

Ace

Alternative uses: Acee, Acer

Origin: Latin

Meaning: best

Achilles

Alternative uses: Achille, Achilleo

Origin: Greek

Meaning: famous fictional Greek warrior

Adam

Alternative uses: Adams

Origin: Hebrew

Meaning: son of the earth

Adrian

Alternative uses: Adrean, Adryan, Adrien

Origin: Latin

Meaning: from Hadria, a large city in Rome

Adriel

Alternative uses: Adri

Origin: Hebrew

Meaning: of God's flock

Adonis

Alternative uses: Adon, Adanis

Origin: Greek

Meaning: incredibly handsome

Ahmed

Alternative uses: Amed

Origin: Arabic

Meaning: highly praised

Aidan

Alternative uses: Aedan, Aiden, Ayden

Origin: Gaelic

Meaning: fire

Ajax

Alternative uses: Jax

Origin: Greek

Meaning: famous fictional Greek warrior

Alan

Alternative uses: Alen, Allen, Allan

Origin: German

Meaning: precious one

Alcott

Alternative uses: Alcot

Origin: British

Meaning: from the old cottage

Amos

Alternative uses: Amis

Origin: Hebrew

Meaning: carried by God

Alexander

Alternative uses: Alex, Alec, Alejandro

Origin: Greek

Meaning: defender of mankind

Anderson

Alternative uses: Anders, Andersen

Origin: Scandinavian

Meaning: son of Andrew

Andrew

Alternative uses: Andy, Andre, Drew

Origin: Greek

Meaning: man, warrior

Angelo

Alternative uses: Angel

Origin: Greek

Meaning: messenger

Anthony

Alternative uses: Antony, Tony, Antonio

Origin: Latin

Meaning: prestigious Roman surname

Amir

Alternative uses: Ameer

Origin: Hebrew

Meaning: prince

Apollo

Alternative uses: Apolo, Pollo

Origin: Greek

Meaning: destroyer, conqueror

Archer

Alternative uses: Arch

Origin: Latin

Meaning: bowman, hunter

Arlo

Alternative uses: Arlow

Origin: Spanish

Meaning: barberry tree

Armando

Alternative uses: Mando, Armie

Origin: German

Meaning: soldier

Arthur

Alternative uses: Art, Arther

Origin: Celtic

Meaning: noble, courageous

Asher

Alternative uses: Ash, Ashby, Ashur

Origin: Hebrew

Meaning: happy

Atlas

Alternative uses: Atlis

Origin: Greek

Meaning: strong carrier

Atticus

Alternative uses: Aticus

Origin: Latin

Meaning: from Athens, center of wisdom

August

Alternative uses: Augustus, Gus, Augie

Origin: Latin

Meaning: great, magnificent

Austin

Alternative uses: Austen

Origin: Latin

Meaning: great, magnificent

B

Bain

Alternative uses: Bane

Origin: Irish

Meaning: pale, from the pale bridge

Banner

Alternative uses: Bann

Origin: French

Meaning: flag bearer

Barker

Alternative uses: Bark, Barkar

Origin: British

Meaning: shepherd

Barrett

Alternative uses: Barratt, Barret, Berrett

Origin: German

Meaning: fighter

Baz

Alternative uses: none

Origin: Irish

Meaning: fair-haired

Bear

Alternative uses: Behr

Origin: German

Meaning: brave and strong

Beau

Alternative uses: Bo

Origin: French

Meaning: beautiful, good-looking

Beckham

Alternative uses: Beck, Bekam

Origin: British

Meaning: lives by the stream

Beckett

Alternative uses: Beck, Becket

Origin: British

Meaning: beehive

Benedict

Alternative uses: Benedick

Origin: Latin

Meaning: blessed

Benjamin

Alternative uses: Ben, Benji, Benjamen

Origin: Hebrew

Meaning: son of the right hand

Bennett

Alternative uses: Benett, Bennet

Origin: Latin

Meaning: blessed

Benson

Alternative uses: Bensen

Origin: British

Meaning: little son of the right hand

Berkeley

Alternative uses: Berkley, Berk

Origin: British

Meaning: lives in the meadow

Blais

Alternative uses: Blaise, Blaze

Origin: French

Meaning: quiet

Blane

Alternative uses: Blaney

Origin: Gaelic

Meaning: golden

Boaz

Alternative uses: none

Origin: Hebrew

Meaning: strength

Bode

Alternative uses: Bowdy, Bowde

Origin: Scandinavian

Meaning: messenger

Bolton

Alternative uses: Bolten, Boltin, Bolt

Origin: British

Meaning: uncertain, possibly a town

Booker

Alternative uses: Bookor

Origin: British

Meaning: scribe, writer

Boone

Alternative uses: Boon

Origin: Latin

Meaning: good, blessing

Booth

Alternative uses: Boothe

Origin: Scandinavian

Meaning: dwelling place

Bowen

Alternative uses: Bowie, Bowin

Origin: Welsh

Meaning: son of the young one

Brandt

Alternative uses: Brant

Origin: Norse

Meaning: sword, fiery torch

Braxton

Alternative uses: Brax

Origin: British

Meaning: Brock's town

Brayden

Alternative uses: Braeden, Braydan

Origin: Irish

Meaning: broad, brave, wise

Brandon

Alternative uses: Brando

Origin: British

Meaning: from the hill

Brendan

Alternative uses: Brennan, Bren

Origin: Irish

Meaning: prince

Brian

Alternative uses: Bryan, Brien

Origin: Irish

Meaning: high, noble

Brock

Alternative uses: Brok, Broc

Origin: British

Meaning: tenacious

Bronson

Alternative uses: Bronsan, Bronn

Origin: British

Meaning: son of the brown man

Bruno

Alternative uses: Brun

Origin: German

Meaning: brown

Bryce

Alternative uses: Brice

Origin: Welsh

Meaning: speckled, freckled

Bryson

Alternative uses: Brison

Origin: Welsh

Meaning: son of Bryce

C

Cabe

Alternative uses: none

Origin: French

Meaning: rope-maker, industrious

Cairo

Alternative uses: Cayro

Origin: Arabic

Meaning: victorious

Cale

Alternative uses: Cael

Origin: British

Meaning: rejoice

Caleb

Alternative uses: Cayleb

Origin: Hebrew

Meaning: faith, devotion

Callum

Alternative uses: Callim

Origin: Scottish

Meaning: dove, gentle

Calvin

Alternative uses: Calven, Cal

Origin: French

Meaning: little bald one

Camden

Alternative uses: Camdin, Cam

Origin: Scottish

Meaning: winding valley

Cameron

Alternative uses: Camron, Cam

Origin: Scottish

Meaning: surname, from the crooked river

Canaan

Alternative uses: Caanin

Origin: Hebrew

Meaning: merchant

Cannon

Alternative uses: Canon

Origin: French

Meaning: official of the church

Carlos

Alternative uses: Carlo, Carlow, Carlowe

Origin: Spanish

Meaning: free man

Casey

Alternative uses: Case

Origin: Irish

Meaning: alert, watchful

Cas

Alternative uses: Cas

Origin: Latin

Meaning: keeper of money

Cayden

Alternative uses: Caiden, Caden, Caydan

Origin: Arabic

Meaning: companion

Cesar

Alternative uses: Caeser, Caesar

Origin: Latin

Meaning: head of hair

Chad

Alternative uses: Chadwick, Chadick

Origin: British

Meaning: protector, defender

Chance

Alternative uses: Chanse

Origin: British

Meaning: good fortune

Chandler

Alternative uses:

Origin: French

Meaning: maker of candles

Charles

Alternative uses: Charley, Charlie, Chuck

Origin: German

Meaning: free man

Chase

Alternative uses: Chace

Origin: French

Meaning: huntsman

Chip

Alternative uses: none

Origin: German

Meaning: free man

Christian

Alternative uses: Cristian

Origin: Greek

Meaning: follower of Christ

Christopher

Alternative uses: Chris, Christofer, Topher

Origin: Greek

Meaning: bearing Christ

Cillian

Alternative uses: Killian

Origin: Irish

Meaning: bright-headed

Cisco

Alternative uses: Sisco

Origin: Spanish

Meaning: Frenchman

Clayton

Alternative uses: Clay

Origin: British

Meaning: settlement made of clay

Clark

Alternative uses: Clarke

Origin: Latin

Meaning: clerk

Clint

Alternative uses: none

Origin: British

Meaning: fenced settlement, protected

Coby

Alternative uses: Cobie, Cobee

Origin: Scottish

Meaning: stream

Colby

Alternative uses: Colbee

Origin: Norse

Meaning: strong man's settlement

Cole

Alternative uses: Col, Coal

Origin: Scottish

Meaning: young creature

Colin

Alternative uses: Colen, Collin

Origin: Scottish

Meaning: young creature

Colton

Alternative uses: Colt, Colten, Colter

Origin: British

Meaning: coal town

Conner

Alternative uses: Connor

Origin: Irish

Meaning: hound-lover

Conrad

Alternative uses: none

Origin: German

Meaning: brave, bold ruler

Cooper

Alternative uses: Coopor, Cowper, Coop

Origin: British

Meaning: barrel maker

Corbin

Alternative uses: Corben, Corbett

Origin: French

Meaning: raven

Court

Alternative uses: Cort

Origin: German

Meaning: land of the brave

Cruz

Alternative uses: Cruze, Cruise

Origin: Spanish

Meaning: cross

Curtis

Alternative uses: Curt, Curtice

Origin: British

Meaning: brave

Cyrus

Alternative uses: Cy, Syrus

Origin: Persian

Meaning: lord, ruler

D

Dalen

Alternative uses: Daylen, Dailan

Origin: British

Meaning: valley

Dalton

Alternative uses: Dalten

Origin: British

Meaning: from the valley town

Damian

Alternative uses: Damien, Damon, Daimon

Origin: Greek

Meaning: subdue

Daniel

Alternative uses: Danny, Danyel

Origin: Hebrew

Meaning: God is my judge

Dante

Alternative uses: Dantay, Dahnte

Origin: Spanish

Meaning: lasting, enduring

Darin

Alternative uses: Darren, Darian

Origin: Irish

Meaning: great

Darius

Alternative uses: Darrius

Origin: Persian

Meaning: keeps his treasures well

Dartagnan

Alternative uses: D'Artagnan, Dart

Origin: French

Meaning: from Artagnan, a town in France

David

Alternative uses: Daved, Dave

Origin: Hebrew

Meaning: beloved

Davis

Alternative uses: Davus

Origin: British

Meaning: son of David

Dawson

Alternative uses: Dawsen, Dawes

Origin: British

Meaning: beloved

Dax

Alternative uses: Daks

Origin: French

Meaning: city in France in the 4th century

Deacon

Alternative uses: Deecon

Origin: Greek

Meaning: messenger, servant

Dean

Alternative uses: Deen, Dene

Origin: British

Meaning: valley

Declan

Alternative uses: Deklan, Deck

Origin: Irish

Meaning: unknown

Demetrius

Alternative uses: Dimetrius, Dem

Origin: Greek

Meaning: serves Demeter, goddess of plenty

Dennis

Alternative uses: Denny, Denis

Origin: Greek

Meaning: serves Dionysius, god of mirth

Derek

Alternative uses: Derrick, Derik, Derreck

Origin: German

Meaning: power of the tribe

Dexter

Alternative uses: Dex

Origin: Latin

Meaning: fortunate

Diego

Alternative uses: none

Origin: Spanish

Meaning: he who supplants

Dirk

Alternative uses: Derk, Dirke

Origin: Dutch

Meaning: famous ruler

Dominic

Alternative uses: Dom, Dominick

Origin: Latin

Meaning: lord, ruler

Donald

Alternative uses: Don

Origin: Scottish

Meaning: mighty

Donovan

Alternative uses: Don, Donavan

Origin: Irish

Meaning: dark ruler, dark-haired ruler

Douglas

Alternative uses: Doug, Douglass

Origin: Scottish

Meaning: black river

Drake

Alternative uses: Drayk

Origin: British

Meaning: dragon

Duke

Alternative uses: none

Origin: Latin

Meaning: leader

Dylan

Alternative uses: Dillon, Dylon

Origin: Welsh

Meaning: like a lion, loyal

E

Easton

Alternative uses: East

Origin: British

Meaning: settlement in the East

Edison

Alternative uses: Ed, Eddison

Origin: British

Meaning: son of Edward

Edmund

Alternative uses: Ed, Edmond, Edmundo

Origin: British

Meaning: wealthy protector

Edward

Alternative uses: Eduardo, Eddie

Origin: British

Meaning: wealthy guard

Eilan

Alternative uses: Eyelan

Origin: Hebrew

Meaning: oak tree, strong

Elias

Alternative uses: Eli, Elijah, Elyas

Origin: Hebrew

Meaning: the Lord is my God

Elliot

Alternative uses: Eliot, Eliot

Origin: Hebrew

Meaning: the Lord is God

Emanuel

Alternative uses: Eman, Emmanuel, Imanuel

Origin: Hebrew

Meaning: God is with us

Emerson

Alternative uses: Emersen

Origin: British

Meaning: son of the powerful

Emmitt

Alternative uses: Em, Emmett

Origin: British

Meaning: universal, powerful, truthful

Emory

Alternative uses: Emery

Origin: British

Meaning: home strength

Enzo

Alternative uses: none

Origin: Italian

Meaning: home ruler

Eric

Alternative uses: Erik, Erich

Origin: Norse

Meaning: ruler

Esau

Alternative uses: Esaw

Origin: Hebrew

Meaning: hairy, manly

Esteban

Alternative uses: Steban, Esteben

Origin: Spanish

Meaning: crown

Ethan

Alternative uses: none

Origin: Hebrew

Meaning: long-lived

Evan

Alternative uses: Evann, Even

Origin: Welsh

Meaning: God is gracious

Everett

Alternative uses: Ev, Ever, Everitt

Origin: British

Meaning: brave and strong

Everly

Alternative uses: Everley, Ev

Origin: British

Meaning: boar meadow

Ezekiel

Alternative uses: Zeke

Origin: Hebrew

Meaning: strength of God

Ezra

Alternative uses: none

Origin: Hebrew

Meaning: helper

F

Felix

Alternative uses: none

Origin: Latin

Meaning: happy, fortunate

Fernando

Alternative uses: Nando, Fernan

Origin: Spanish

Meaning: adventurer

Fidel

Alternative uses: none

Origin: Latin

Meaning: faithful

Filip

Alternative uses: Fil, Philipp, Phil

Origin: Spanish

Meaning: lover of horses

Finley

Alternative uses: Finnley, Finn

Origin: Irish

Meaning: courageous one

Finnegan

Alternative uses: Finn

Origin: Irish

Meaning: fair, light-haired

Fisher

Alternative uses: none

Origin: British

Meaning: fisherman

Fitzgerald

Alternative uses: Fitz

Origin: German

Meaning: son of the spear-ruler

Fletcher

Alternative uses: Fletch

Origin: British

Meaning: arrow-maker

Floyd

Alternative uses: none

Origin: Welsh

Meaning: gray-haired, wise

Flynn

Alternative uses: Flyn, Flinn

Origin: Irish

Meaning: ruddy complexion, strong

Ford

Alternative uses: none

Origin: British

Meaning: river crossing

Forrest

Alternative uses: Forest

Origin: French

Meaning: woodsman

Foster

Alternative uses: none

Origin: British

Meaning: woodsman

Fox

Alternative uses: none

Origin: British

Meaning: a fox, cunning

Franklin

Alternative uses: Frank, Franklyn

Origin: British

Meaning: free

Francisco

Alternative uses: Fransisco, Cisco

Origin: Spanish

Meaning: Frenchman

G

Gabriel

Alternative uses: Gabe, Gabrielli

Origin: Hebrew

Meaning: hero of God

Gage

Alternative uses: none

Origin: French

Meaning: pledge, oath

Galen

Alternative uses: Gale, Galin

Origin: Greek

Meaning: calm

Garrett

Alternative uses: Garett, Garreth

Origin: British

Meaning: rules by the spear

Gavin

Alternative uses: Gaven, Gav

Origin: Welsh

Meaning: white falcon

Geoffrey

Alternative uses: Geoff, Jeffrey

Origin: German

Meaning: peace

George

Alternative uses: Georg, Georges, Gorgie

Origin: Greek

Meaning: farmer

Gideon

Alternative uses: none

Origin: Hebrew

Meaning: powerful warrior

Gilbert

Alternative uses: Gil, Gill, Gillbert

Origin: French

Meaning: bright promise

Giovanni

Alternative uses: Gio

Origin: Italian

Meaning: God is gracious

Gordon

Alternative uses: Gord, Gordy

Origin: Scottish

Meaning: large fortification, strong

Grady

Alternative uses: Grade, Gradie

Origin: Irish

Meaning: renowned

Graham

Alternative uses: Gram

Origin: British

Meaning: gray homestead

Grant

Alternative uses: none

Origin: Scottish

Meaning: tall, big

Grayson

Alternative uses: Gray, Grey, Greyson

Origin: British

Meaning: late blessing, son of gray man

Gregory

Alternative uses: Greg, Gregori, Gregor

Origin: Greek

Meaning: watchful, vigilant

Griffin

Alternative uses: Griff, Gryffon, Gryphon

Origin: Latin

Meaning: powerful creature

Guillermo

Alternative uses: Guill

Origin: German

Meaning: protection

Gunner

Alternative uses: Gunnar, Gunn

Origin: German

Meaning: battler

H

Hall

Alternative uses: none

Origin: British

Meaning: worker

Hakeem

Alternative uses: Keem

Origin: Arabic

Meaning: wise, intelligent

Hank

Alternative uses: none

Origin: German

Meaning: home ruler

Harlan

Alternative uses: none

Origin: British

Meaning: army land

Harlow

Alternative uses: Harlo

Origin: British

Meaning: army hill

Harper

Alternative uses: Harp

Origin: British

Meaning: minstrel

Harrison

Alternative uses: Harry, Harris

Origin: German

Meaning: son of the ruler

Hartley

Alternative uses: Hart, Hartly, Hartlee

Origin: British

Meaning: stag meadow

Hayden

Alternative uses: Haydon, Haydan, Hayes

Origin: British

Meaning: hedged valley

Heathcliff

Alternative uses: Heath

Origin: British

Meaning: untamed nature

Henry

Alternative uses: Henri

Origin: German

Meaning: home ruler

Hewitt

Alternative uses: Hew, Hewit, Hewett

Origin: French

Meaning: small intelligent one

Hezekiah

Alternative uses: Hez, Hezekieh

Origin: Hebrew

Meaning: God gives strength

Holden

Alternative uses: Hold, Holdin

Origin: British

Meaning: deep valley

Holt

Alternative uses: Holte

Origin: British

Meaning: forest

Houston

Alternative uses: Huston

Origin: Irish

Meaning: town on the hill

Hudson

Alternative uses: Hud, Huddson

Origin: British

Meaning: explorer

Hugh

Alternative uses: Hu, Hue

Origin: German

Meaning: soul, mind, intellect

Hugo

Alternative uses: none

Origin: Latin

Meaning: intelligence

Huxley

Alternative uses: Hux, Hucks

Origin: British

Meaning: meadow

I

Ian

Alternative uses: Iann, Ioan, Ion

Origin: Scottish

Meaning: God is gracious

Ilan

Alternative uses: none

Origin: Hebrew

Meaning: tree

Indio

Alternative uses: Indi, Indy, Indyo

Origin: Spanish

Meaning: native

Irving

Alternative uses: Irvin, Irven, Irvine

Origin: Gaelic

Meaning: fresh water

Ishmael

Alternative uses: Ismael

Origin: Hebrew

Meaning: God listens

Isaac

Alternative uses: Isac, Isaak, Isacco

Origin: Hebrew

Meaning: laughter

Isaiah

Alternative uses: Isaias, Is

Origin: Hebrew

Meaning: salvation of God

Israel

Alternative uses: none

Origin: Hebrew

Meaning: God perseveres

Ivan

Alternative uses: Ive, Ivann, Ivano, Iven

Origin: Slavic

Meaning: God is gracious

J

Jace

Alternative uses: Jase, Jayse, Jayce

Origin: Hebrew

Meaning: healer

Jacob

Alternative uses: Jake, Jakob, Jacoby

Origin: Hebrew

Meaning: trickster, clever

Jackson

Alternative uses: Jaxon, Jacksen, Jack, Jax

Origin: Hebrew

Meaning: son of a gracious God

Jacques

Alternative uses: none

Origin: French

Meaning: God is gracious

Jaden

Alternative uses: Jayden, Jaydan, Jadin

Origin: Hebrew

Meaning: thankful

Jaelan

Alternative uses: Jalen, Jaelen

Origin: American

Meaning: calm

Jair

Alternative uses: Jahr, Jer

Origin: Spanish

Meaning: God enlightens

Jamel

Alternative uses: Jamell

Origin: Arabic

Meaning: handsome

James

Alternative uses: Jaymes, Jamie, Seamus

Origin: Hebrew

Meaning: he who supplants

Jameson

Alternative uses: Jamison

Origin: British

Meaning: son of James

Jason

Alternative uses: Jayson

Origin: Hebrew

Meaning: healer, the Lord is salvation

Jasper

Alternative uses: none

Origin: Greek

Meaning: treasurer

Jeffrey

Alternative uses: Jeff, Jefferey

Origin: German

Meaning: peace

Jefferson

Alternative uses: Jeffersen

Origin: British

Meaning: son of peace

Jens

Alternative uses: none

Origin: Scandinavian

Meaning: God is gracious

Jeremiah

Alternative uses: Jerry, Jeremyah

Origin: Hebrew

Meaning: the Lord exalts

Jeremy

Alternative uses: Jereme, Jere

Origin: American

Meaning: the Lord exalts

Jerome

Alternative uses: Jarome, Jerohm

Origin: Greek

Meaning: sacred name

Jesse

Alternative uses: Jese, Jess

Origin: Hebrew

Meaning: gift

Jesus

Alternative uses: Haysus, Hesus

Origin: Hebrew

Meaning: the Lord is salvation

Joel

Alternative uses: Jole

Origin: Hebrew

Meaning: Jehovah is the Lord

John

Alternative uses: Jon, Johnny, Jonny

Origin: Hebrew

Meaning: God is gracious

Jonah

Alternative uses: Jonas, Jona

Origin: Hebrew

Meaning: dove

Jonathon

Alternative uses: Johnathon, Jon

Origin: Hebrew

Meaning: gift of God

Jordan

Alternative uses: Jordann, Jordon

Origin: Hebrew

Meaning: down-flowing

Joseph

Alternative uses: Joe, Josef

Origin: Hebrew

Meaning: the Lord increases

Joshua

Alternative uses: Josh

Origin: Hebrew

Meaning: the Lord is salvation

Juan

Alternative uses: none

Origin: Spanish

Meaning: God is gracious

Judah

Alternative uses: Jude

Origin: Hebrew

Meaning: praised

Judson

Alternative uses: Judsen, Judd, Jud

Origin: Greek

Meaning: praised

Julian

Alternative uses: Julien, Jules, Jule

Origin: Greek

Meaning: Jove's (Zeus') child

Justin

Alternative uses: Justen, Just, Justyn

Origin: Latin

Meaning: upright, righteous

K

Kadeem

Alternative uses: Kadim, Kad

Origin: Arabic

Meaning: servant

Kael

Alternative uses: Kale, Cale

Origin: Gaelic

Meaning: fair

Kaemon

Alternative uses: Kayman, Caemon

Origin: Japanese

Meaning: joyful

Kairn

Alternative uses: Cairn

Origin: Scottish

Meaning: mound of rocks

Kamal

Alternative uses: Kam, Camal

Origin: Arabic

Meaning: perfection

Karl

Alternative uses: Carl

Origin: German

Meaning: free man

Karr

Alternative uses: Kar, Carr

Origin: Scandinavian

Meaning: from the marshes

Kassim

Alternative uses: Kaseem

Origin: Arabic

Meaning: divided

Keagan

Alternative uses: Keagen, Keegan

Origin: Irish

Meaning: small flame

Kean

Alternative uses: Keane, Keen

Origin: Irish

Meaning: fighter

Kearney

Alternative uses: Kerney, Kearny, Carney

Origin: Irish

Meaning: winner

Keaton

Alternative uses: Keat, Keats, Keaten

Origin: British

Meaning: place of hawks

Keenan

Alternative uses: Kenan, Keenen

Origin: Irish

Meaning: ancient

Keir

Alternative uses: Keer, Kere

Origin: Gaelic

Meaning: dark-haired

Keith

Alternative uses: none

Origin: Scottish

Meaning: woodland

Keller

Alternative uses: Kell

Origin: German

Meaning: cellar

Kelly

Alternative uses: Kel, Kelley

Origin: Irish

Meaning: descendant

Kenneth

Alternative uses: Ken, Keneth

Origin: Scottish

Meaning: fire born

Kern

Alternative uses: Kearn, Kearne

Origin: Irish

Meaning: small swarthy one

Kevin

Alternative uses: Keven, Kev

Origin: Irish

Meaning: handsome

Kiefer

Alternative uses: Keifer, Keefer

Origin: German

Meaning: barrel maker

King

Alternative uses: none

Origin: British

Meaning: king

Kinney

Alternative uses: Kinny, Kin

Origin: Irish

Meaning: good-looking

Kip

Alternative uses: none

Origin: British

Meaning: pointed hill

Kirk

Alternative uses: Kerk

Origin: Norse

Meaning: church

Knox

Alternative uses: Nox, Knocks

Origin: British

Meaning: round-top hill

Kobe

Alternative uses: Kobi, Cobi, Cobe

Origin: Hungarian

Meaning: he who supplants

Kody

Alternative uses: Cody, Coedy

Origin: British

Meaning: helpful

Kyle

Alternative uses: Cyle, Kyl

Origin: Gaelic

Meaning: straight, narrow

L

Lachlan

Alternative uses: Laklan, Lach

Origin: Irish

Meaning: from the lake

Ladd

Alternative uses: Lad

Origin: British

Meaning: manservant

Lado

Alternative uses: none

Origin: unknown

Meaning: unknown

Lake

Alternative uses: Layk

Origin: unknown

Meaning: body of water

Lamar

Alternative uses: Lamer, Lamor

Origin: German

Meaning: the water

Lamont

Alternative uses: LaMont

Origin: Norse

Meaning: lawman

Lance

Alternative uses: Lanz, Lanse

Origin: French

Meaning: land

Landon

Alternative uses: Landen, Lan

Origin: British

Meaning: long hill

Lane

Alternative uses: Lain, Laine

Origin: British

Meaning: path

Lark

Alternative uses: none

Origin: British

Meaning: playful

Larry

Alternative uses: none

Origin: British

Meaning: unknown

Lars

Alternative uses: Larrs

Origin: Scandinavian

Meaning: unknown

Lawson

Alternative uses: Laws, Law, Lawsen

Origin: British

Meaning: son of Lawrence

Lazlo

Alternative uses: Laslo, Lazlow

Origin: Slavic

Meaning: glorious rule

Leander

Alternative uses: Lee, Leandar

Origin: Greek

Meaning: lion man

Leary

Alternative uses: Learey, Lear, Leer

Origin: Irish

Meaning: herder

Leeland

Alternative uses: Lee, Leelend

Origin: British

Meaning: one who lives by raw land

Leif

Alternative uses: Leef

Origin: Scandinavian

Meaning: beloved heir

Lemar

Alternative uses: Lamar

Origin: German

Meaning: the water

Lennox

Alternative uses: Len, Lenn

Origin: Scottish

Meaning: many elm trees

Leo

Alternative uses: none

Origin: Latin

Meaning: lion

Levi

Alternative uses: Lev, Levy

Origin: Hebrew

Meaning: joined

Liam

Alternative uses: Lyam, Liamm

Origin: German

Meaning: protection

Lincoln

Alternative uses: Linc, Link, Linkoln

Origin: British

Meaning: Lake Colony

Linton

Alternative uses: Lynton, Lint

Origin: British

Meaning: flax settlement

Lionel

Alternative uses: Lio, Lion, Lyonel

Origin: Latin

Meaning: lion

Lloyd

Alternative uses: Loyd

Origin: Welsh

Meaning: sacred

Lock

Alternative uses: Lok

Origin: German

Meaning: fortified place

Logan

Alternative uses: none

Origin: Scottish

Meaning: hollow, valley

London

Alternative uses: Londyn, Lond

Origin: unknown

Meaning: a place in England

Lope

Alternative uses: none

Origin: unknown

Meaning: unknown

Louis

Alternative uses: Lou, Lew, Lewis, Louie

Origin: Latin

Meaning: famous warrior

Lucas

Alternative uses: Luc, Luca

Origin: German

Meaning: light

Luke

Alternative uses: Lewk, Luc

Origin: Greek

Meaning: light

Luther

Alternative uses: Luth, Luthur. Luthor

Origin: German

Meaning: soldier of the people

Lyle

Alternative uses: none

Origin: French

Meaning: island

Lyndon

Alternative uses: Linton, Lynton, Linden

Origin: British

Meaning: tree hill

M

Mac

Alternative uses: Mak, Mack

Origin: Gaelic

Meaning: son

Mackenzie

Alternative uses: McKenzie, Mackenze

Origin: Irish

Meaning: son of a wise ruler

Maddox

Alternative uses: Madox, Maddoks

Origin: Welsh

Meaning: benefactor's son

Malachi

Alternative uses: Malakye, Malaki

Origin: Hebrew

Meaning: messenger of God

Manuel

Alternative uses: Manwell

Origin: Spanish

Meaning: God is with us

March

Alternative uses: none

Origin: French

Meaning: frontier

Marco

Alternative uses: Marko

Origin: Latin

Meaning: warlike

Marcus

Alternative uses: Markus, Marqus

Origin: Latin

Meaning: dedicated to Mars, god of war

Mariner

Alternative uses: Mar

Origin: British

Meaning: sailor

Marius

Alternative uses: Mareus

Origin: Latin

Meaning: manly

Mark

Alternative uses: Marc, Marq

Origin: Latin

Meaning: dedicated to Mars, god of war

Marley

Alternative uses: Marly

Origin: British

Meaning: meadow near the lake

Marshall

Alternative uses: Marshal, Marsh

Origin: French

Meaning: caretaker

Martin

Alternative uses: Marten, Martyn

Origin: Latin

Meaning: dedicated to Mars, god of war

Mateo

Alternative uses: Matayo

Origin: Hebrew

Meaning: gift of God

Matthew

Alternative uses: Mathieu, Matt

Origin: Hebrew

Meaning: gift of God

Matthias

Alternative uses: Mathias

Origin: Welsh

Meaning: gift of God

Maximillian

Alternative uses: Max

Origin: Latin

Meaning: greatest

McKinley

Alternative uses: Mackinly, Mckinly

Origin: Scottish

Meaning: learned ruler

Merrick

Alternative uses: Meuric, Marick, Merick

Origin: Welsh

Meaning: powerful

Merritt

Alternative uses: Merrett, Merit

Origin: British

Meaning: boundary gate

Micah

Alternative uses: Mikah, Micha, Mica

Origin: Hebrew

Meaning: who is like God?

Michael

Alternative uses: Mike, Mikael

Origin: Hebrew

Meaning: who is like God?

Miguel

Alternative uses: Mig

Origin: Hebrew

Meaning: who is like God?

Miles

Alternative uses: Myles

Origin: British

Meaning: soldier

Miller

Alternative uses: Miler, Mill

Origin: British

Meaning: one who grinds grain

Milo

Alternative uses: Mylo

Origin: British

Meaning: soldier

Mitchell

Alternative uses: Mitch, Mitchel

Origin: Hebrew

Meaning: who is like God?

Moise

Alternative uses: Moises, Moishe

Origin: Hebrew

Meaning: savior

Montgomery

Alternative uses: Mont, Monty

Origin: French

Meaning: large hill

Moses

Alternative uses: Mose

Origin: Hebrew

Meaning: savior

Muhammad

Alternative uses: Mohammad, Muhamet

Origin: Arabic

Meaning: praiseworthy

Murphy

Alternative uses: Murph, Murphey, Murphay

Origin: Irish

Meaning: sea warrior

Murray

Alternative uses: Murry

Origin: Gaelic

Meaning: lord, master

N

Naphatali

Alternative uses: Naph, Naftali, Naf

Origin: Hebrew

Meaning: struggle

Nash

Alternative uses: none

Origin: British

Meaning: ash tree, protector

Nasir

Alternative uses: Nas, Naseer

Origin: Arabic

Meaning: supporter

Nathan

Alternative uses: Nate

Origin: Hebrew

Meaning: God has given

Nathaniel

Alternative uses: Nathanial, Nathanyel

Origin: Hebrew

Meaning: God has given

Nehemiah

Alternative uses: Nehimiah, Miah

Origin: Hebrew

Meaning: comforter

Neil

Alternative uses: Neal, Neel

Origin: Scottish

Meaning: champion

Nelson

Alternative uses: Nels, Nelsen

Origin: British

Meaning: champion

Nestor

Alternative uses: Nes, Nester

Origin: Greek

Meaning: traveler

Nevin

Alternative uses: Nev, Neven

Origin: Latin

Meaning: holy, sacred

Niall

Alternative uses: Nyall, Neeal

Origin: Irish

Meaning: champion

Nicholas

Alternative uses: Nick, Nic, Nickolas

Origin: Greek

Meaning: people of victory

Nigel

Alternative uses: Nig, Nigal, Nygel

Origin: Spanish

Meaning: champion

Nike

Alternative uses: Niki

Origin: Greek

Meaning: victory

Niles

Alternative uses: Nyles

Origin: Irish

Meaning: cloud

Noah

Alternative uses: Noa

Origin: Hebrew

Meaning: peaceful

Noam

Alternative uses: none

Origin: Hebrew

Meaning: beautiful

Noble

Alternative uses: Nob, Nobel

Origin: Latin

Meaning: aristocratic

Norman

Alternative uses: Norm

Origin: German

Meaning: from the North

North

Alternative uses: none

Origin: unknown

Meaning: North

O

Oak

Alternative uses: Oke, Oakes

Origin: British

Meaning: oak tree

Oakley

Alternative uses: Oakly, Oaklee, Oakleigh

Origin: British

Meaning: meadow of oak trees

Obadiah

Alternative uses: Obi, Obidiah

Origin: Hebrew

Meaning: servant of God

Obed

Alternative uses: none

Origin: Hebrew

Meaning: servant of God

Oberon

Alternative uses: Obe, Obi, Beron

Origin: German

Meaning: royal bear

Octavio

Alternative uses: Octo, Octavius, Octave

Origin: Latin

Meaning: eighth

Odin

Alternative uses: Odi, Oden

Origin: Norse

Meaning: for Odin, god of death and art

Olen

Alternative uses: Olin

Origin: British

Meaning: relic

Oliver

Alternative uses: Ollie, Olivir, Olivier

Origin: Latin

Meaning: olive tree

Omar

Alternative uses: none

Origin: Persian

Meaning: flourishing

Orin

Alternative uses: Oren, Oran

Origin: Irish

Meaning: light, fair

Orion

Alternative uses: none

Origin: Greek

Meaning: for Orion, might hunter

Orlando

Alternative uses: Orlan, Orlondo

Origin: Spanish

Meaning: famous land

Orville

Alternative uses: Orvie, Orvil

Origin: French

Meaning: gold town

Oscar

Alternative uses: Oskar

Origin: British

Meaning: spear of the gods

Otis

Alternative uses: Otes, Oti

Origin: German

Meaning: wealth

Owen

Alternative uses: Owin, Owain

Origin: Welsh

Meaning: youth

P

Pablo

Alternative uses: none

Origin: Spanish

Meaning: little

Pace

Alternative uses: Pase, Payce

Origin: Hebrew

Meaning: peace

Packer

Alternative uses: Paker, Pack, Pac

Origin: unknown

Meaning: brave, strong

Palmer

Alternative uses: Palmar

Origin: British

Meaning: pilgrim

Paolo

Alternative uses: Paol

Origin: Latin

Meaning: small

Parker

Alternative uses: Park, Parks

Origin: British

Meaning: keeper

Pasquale

Alternative uses: Pasq, Pas, Pascal

Origin: Latin

Meaning: Easter child

Patrick

Alternative uses: Pat, Patric

Origin: Latin

Meaning: noble

Patton

Alternative uses: Paton, Patten, Pattan

Origin: British

Meaning: fighter's town

Paul

Alternative uses: Pol

Origin: Latin

Meaning: small

Paxton

Alternative uses: Pax, Packston

Origin: British

Meaning: peaceful

Pearson

Alternative uses: Pierson, Pearsan

Origin: Greek

Meaning: rock

Pedro

Alternative uses: Piedro, Ped

Origin: Spanish

Meaning: rock

Pell

Alternative uses: Pel

Origin: British

Meaning: parchment

Penn

Alternative uses: Pen

Origin: British

Meaning: hill

Percy

Alternative uses: Perce, Percie

Origin: Latin

Meaning: hunter

Perseus

Alternative uses: Pers, Persius

Origin: Greek

Meaning: for Perseus, slayer of Medusa

Peter

Alternative uses: Pete, Petre, Pyotr, Pieter

Origin: Greek

Meaning: rock

Philip

Alternative uses: Phil, Filip

Origin: Greek

Meaning: lover of horses

Phineas

Alternative uses: Fineas, Phin, Fin

Origin: Hebrew

Meaning: oracle

Pierce

Alternative uses: Pierc, Piers

Origin: Greek

Meaning: rock

Pierre

Alternative uses: Piere

Origin: French

Meaning: rock

Platt

Alternative uses: Plat

Origin: French

Meaning: flat land

Porter

Alternative uses: Portor, Port

Origin: French

Meaning: gatekeeper

Prentice

Alternative uses: Prentiss, Prentis

Origin: British

Meaning: apprentice

Prescott

Alternative uses: Prescot

Origin: British

Meaning: priest's cottage

Presley

Alternative uses: Presly, Pressley

Origin: British

Meaning: priest's meadow

Preston

Alternative uses: Prestin, Pres

Origin: British

Meaning: priest's town

Prewitt

Alternative uses: Pruitt, Prew, Pru

Origin: French

Meaning: brave little one

Prince

Alternative uses: Prins

Origin: Latin

Meaning: prince

Q

Qasim

Alternative uses: Kasim, Quaseem, Quasim

Origin: Arabic

Meaning: generous

Quade

Alternative uses: none

Origin: Gaelic

Meaning: born fourth

Quent

Alternative uses: Quen, Quint

Origin: Latin

Meaning: fifth

Quillen

Alternative uses: Quill, Quillin

Origin: Irish

Meaning: cub

Quinton

Alternative uses: Quint, Quinten, Quintin

Origin: British

Meaning: queen's settlement

Quinto

Alternative uses: none

Origin: unknown

Meaning: fifth-born son

R

Rab

Alternative uses: none

Origin: German

Meaning: bright fame

Radley

Alternative uses: Radleigh, Radly

Origin: British

Meaning: red meadow

Rafael

Alternative uses: Rafe, Rafel, Raf

Origin: Spanish

Meaning: God has healed

Rahm

Alternative uses: none

Origin: Sanskrit

Meaning: pleasing

Raines

Alternative uses: Rains, Raine, Rain, Rane

Origin: British

Meaning: lord

Ralph

Alternative uses: Ralf

Origin: British

Meaning: wolf counsel

Ramone

Alternative uses: Ramon

Origin: Spanish

Meaning: protecting hands

Ramzi

Alternative uses: Ramsi, Ramsey, Ramsay

Origin: British

Meaning: island

Randall

Alternative uses: Rand, Randal

Origin: German

Meaning: wolf shield

Ransom

Alternative uses: Rans, Ran

Origin: British

Meaning: warrior's shield

Rasheed

Alternative uses: Rashid

Origin: Arabic

Meaning: rightly guided

Raymond

Alternative uses: Ray, Ramond

Origin: German

Meaning: protecting hands

Reagen

Alternative uses: Ragen, Regan

Origin: Gaelic

Meaning: little ruler

Reardon

Alternative uses: Rearden, Reardan

Origin: Irish

Meaning: bard

Reeve

Alternative uses: Reev

Origin: British

Meaning: bailiff

Reinhart

Alternative uses: Rinehart, Reinart

Origin: German

Meaning: brave counsel

Reid

Alternative uses: Reed

Origin: British

Meaning: red-haired

Remington

Alternative uses: Remi, Rem

Origin: British

Meaning: raven

Reuben

Alternative uses: Ruben, Rube, Rubio

Origin: Hebrew

Meaning: a son

Rex

Alternative uses: none

Origin: Latin

Meaning: king

Rhett

Alternative uses: Rett, Ret

Origin: Latin

Meaning: speaker

Rhys

Alternative uses: Reece, Reese

Origin: Welsh

Meaning: enthusiasm

Richard

Alternative uses: Rich, Rick, Rickard

Origin: German

Meaning: powerful leader

Riddley

Alternative uses: Ridley, Riddly, Ridly

Origin: British

Meaning: reed meadow

River

Alternative uses: Rivre, Rive, Rivers

Origin: British

Meaning: flowing body of water

Roald

Alternative uses: none

Origin: Norse

Meaning: famous ruler

Robert

Alternative uses: Rob, Robb, Robbert

Origin: German

Meaning: bright fame

Rocco

Alternative uses: Roko, Rocko

Origin: Italian

Meaning: rest, peace

Roderick

Alternative uses: Rodrick, Rodderick

Origin: German

Meaning: famous power

Rodger

Alternative uses: Roger

Origin: German

Meaning: famous spearman

Rodney

Alternative uses: Rodny, Rod, Roddy

Origin: German

Meaning: island near the clearing

Roland

Alternative uses: Rolan, Rol

Origin: German

Meaning: renowned land

Romeo

Alternative uses: Romio, Romi, Rome

Origin: Italian

Meaning: unknown

Ronald

Alternative uses: Ron

Origin: Norse

Meaning: ruler's counselor

Ronin

Alternative uses: Ronan, Ronen, Roanin

Origin: German

Meaning: well-advised ruler

Rorey

Alternative uses: Rory

Origin: Irish

Meaning: red king

Roscoe

Alternative uses: Rosco, Ros

Origin: Norse

Meaning: deer wood

Rourke

Alternative uses: Rorke

Origin: Irish

Meaning: uncertain

Rush

Alternative uses: none

Origin: British

Meaning: dwells by the rushes

Russell

Alternative uses: Russ, Russel

Origin: French

Meaning: little red

Ryan

Alternative uses: none

Origin: Gaelic

Meaning: king

Ryder

Alternative uses: Rider, Ryd, Ry

Origin: British

Meaning: horseman

S

Saeed

Alternative uses: Said

Origin: Arabic

Meaning: happy

Saint

Alternative uses: none

Origin: Latin

Meaning: holy

Salem

Alternative uses: Sal, Saylem

Origin: Hebrew

Meaning: peace

Salvador

Alternative uses: Sal, Salvatore, Salvidor

Origin: Latin

Meaning: savior

Samir

Alternative uses: Sameer

Origin: Sanskrit

Meaning: gust of wind

Samson

Alternative uses: Sam, Samsen

Origin: Hebrew

Meaning: sun

Samuel

Alternative uses: Sam, Samwell

Origin: Hebrew

Meaning: God heard

Sanders

Alternative uses: Sander

Origin: British

Meaning: son of Alexander

Santiago

Alternative uses: Santi, Sant

Origin: Spanish

Meaning: for Saint James

Saul

Alternative uses: Sol

Origin: Hebrew

Meaning: prayed for

Saxon

Alternative uses: Sax, Sacks, Sackson

Origin: German

Meaning: from Saxony

Sawyer

Alternative uses: none

Origin: British

Meaning: wood-worker

Sayers

Alternative uses: none

Origin: Welsh

Meaning: wood-worker

Schaeffer

Alternative uses: Shaffer, Shaeffer, Schaef

Origin: German

Meaning: steward

Scott

Alternative uses: Scot, Scotty

Origin: British

Meaning: from Scotland

Seamus

Alternative uses: Shaymus

Origin: Irish

Meaning: he who supplants

Sean

Alternative uses: Shawn, Shaun

Origin: Irish

Meaning: God is gracious

Sebastian

Alternative uses: Bas, Sebastian, Bastian

Origin: Greek

Meaning: revered

Seeley

Alternative uses: Seely

Origin: French

Meaning: blessed

Selah

Alternative uses: none

Origin: Hebrew

Meaning: boulder or cliff

Sergio

Alternative uses: Serg, Serjio

Origin: Latin

Meaning: servant

Seth

Alternative uses: none

Origin: Hebrew

Meaning: appointed

Shad

Alternative uses: none

Origin: Hebrew

Meaning: miracle

Sheldon

Alternative uses: none

Origin: British

Meaning: steep valley

Shepherd

Alternative uses: Shep, Shepard

Origin: British

Meaning: shepherd

Sherman

Alternative uses: Sherm

Origin: British

Meaning: shearman

Shia

Alternative uses: Shya, Shy, Shi

Origin: Hebrew

Meaning: praise God

Sid

Alternative uses: Syd

Origin: British

Meaning: wide meadow

Silas

Alternative uses: Sylas, Si

Origin: Latin

Meaning: forest

Silvano

Alternative uses: Silvanus, Silv

Origin: Latin

Meaning: woods

Simon

Alternative uses: Sim, Simeon

Origin: Hebrew

Meaning: to hear

Sinclair

Alternative uses: Sin, Sinclare, Sinclar

Origin: British

Meaning: from Saint-Clair, a city in France

Skip

Alternative uses: none

Origin: British

Meaning: ship

Skylar

Alternative uses: Skyler, Schuyler, Sky

Origin: Danish

Meaning: fugitive

Slater

Alternative uses: Slate, Slayter

Origin: British

Meaning: hewer of stone

Smith

Alternative uses: Smit, Smyth

Origin: British

Meaning: metalworker

Solomon

Alternative uses: Sol, Solamon

Origin: Hebrew

Meaning: peace

Soren

Alternative uses: Sorin

Origin: Danish

Meaning: serious

Spiro

Alternative uses: Speero, Spir, Spere

Origin: Greek

Meaning: basket

Stanten

Alternative uses: Stan, Stanton

Origin: British

Meaning: stone settlement

Stark

Alternative uses: none

Origin: German

Meaning: strong

Stef

Alternative uses: Steph

Origin: Greek

Meaning: crown

Sterling

Alternative uses: Stirling, Ster

Origin: British

Meaning: genuine

Steven

Alternative uses: Steve, Stephen

Origin: Greek

Meaning: crown

Stewart

Alternative uses: Stew, Stuart, Stu

Origin: British

Meaning: steward

Sullivan

Alternative uses: Sully

Origin: Gaelic

Meaning: dark eyes

Sutton

Alternative uses: Sutt, Sutten

Origin: British

Meaning: from the South

Sylvester

Alternative uses: Syl, Silvester

Origin: Latin

Meaning: wooded

T

Tadeus

Alternative uses: Tad, Tadius

Origin: unknown

Meaning: unknown

Taggert
Alternative uses: Taggart, Tag
Origin: Irish
Meaning: son of the priest

Tai
Alternative uses: Ty, Tie
Origin: unknown
Meaning: unknown

Taine
Alternative uses: Tayne, Tain
Origin: unknown
Meaning: unknown

Taj
Alternative uses: none
Origin: Sanskrit
Meaning: crown

Talbert
Alternative uses: Tal, Talb, Talbart
Origin: unknown
Meaning: an aristocratic surname

Talon
Alternative uses: Tal, Talen, Talin
Origin: French
Meaning: sharp

Tamir
Alternative uses: Tam, Tameer
Origin: Hebrew
Meaning: erect, tall

Tanner
Alternative uses: Tan, Tannar
Origin: British
Meaning: leather maker

Taos
Alternative uses: none
Origin: unknown
Meaning: unknown

Tareeq
Alternative uses: Tariq
Origin: Arabic
Meaning: evening caller

Taurus
Alternative uses: Torus, Taurus
Origin: Latin
Meaning: bull

Tavenner
Alternative uses: Tav, Tavener
Origin: British
Meaning: tavern-keeper

Taylor
Alternative uses: Tayler, Tailor, Tay
Origin: French
Meaning: tailor

Taz
Alternative uses: Tas
Origin: American
Meaning: unknown

Temp
Alternative uses: none
Origin: British
Meaning: temple

Tennessee
Alternative uses: Ten, Tenny, Tenisee
Origin: Native American
Meaning: unknown, state name

Thaddeus
Alternative uses: Thad, Tad, Taddeus

Origin: Aramaic

Meaning: heart

Thane

Alternative uses: Thayn

Origin: Scottish

Meaning: landholder

Thatcher

Alternative uses: Thatch

Origin: British

Meaning: roof thatcher

Theodore

Alternative uses: Theo, Ted, Teddy, Theodor

Origin: Greek

Meaning: God's gift

Thomas

Alternative uses: Tomas, Tom, Tommy

Origin: Aramaic

Meaning: twin

Thor

Alternative uses: none

Origin: Norse

Meaning: thunder

Thorn

Alternative uses: Thorne

Origin: British

Meaning: thorn bush

Tiesen

Alternative uses: Thiessen, Tiessen

Origin: French

Meaning: high-spirited

Timothy

Alternative uses: Tim, Timmy

Origin: Greek

Meaning: God's honor

Tin

Alternative uses: Tyn

Origin: unknown

Meaning: unknown

Titus

Alternative uses: Tytus, Ty

Origin: Latin

Meaning: honor

Tobias

Alternative uses: Toby, Tobius, Tobi

Origin: Hebrew

Meaning: God is good

Todd

Alternative uses: Tod

Origin: British

Meaning: fox

Travis

Alternative uses: Traves

Origin: French

Meaning: to cross over

Trenton

Alternative uses: Trent, Trenten

Origin: British

Meaning: Trent's town

Trevor

Alternative uses: Trev, Trever

Origin: Welsh

Meaning: great settlement

Trey

Alternative uses: Tre, Tray

Origin: British

Meaning: three

Trip

Alternative uses: none

Origin: unknown

Meaning: unknown

Tristan

Alternative uses: Tris, Trystan, Tristen

Origin: Celtic

Meaning: sad

Troy

Alternative uses: none

Origin: Irish

Meaning: footsoldier

Truman

Alternative uses: Tru, Trumen

Origin: British

Meaning: loyal one

Tuck

Alternative uses: Tuk

Origin: British

Meaning: garment maker

Turk

Alternative uses: none

Origin: British

Meaning: from Turkey

Twain

Alternative uses: Twane

Origin: British

Meaning: divided into two

Tye

Alternative uses: Ty

Origin: British

Meaning: unknown

Tyrone

Alternative uses: Tyron, Tyroan

Origin: Gaelic

Meaning: Owen's country

U

Ulysses

Alternative uses: Ulyses, Ulys

Origin: Latin

Meaning: for the hero of *Odyssey*

Umar

Alternative uses: Umer

Origin: Arabic

Meaning: thriving

Umber

Alternative uses: none

Origin: French

Meaning: shade

Umberto

Alternative uses: none

Origin: Italian

Meaning: unknown

Urban

Alternative uses: Urb, Urbin, Urben, Urbane

Origin: Latin

Meaning: from the city

Uriah

Alternative uses: Uria, Urijah

Origin: Hebrew

Meaning: my light is Jehovah

Uriel

Alternative uses: none

Origin: Hebrew

Meaning: angel of light

Urson

Alternative uses: Orson, Ursen, Orsen

Origin: Latin

Meaning: bear

Uzziah

Alternative uses: Uziah, Uzzia

Origin: Hebrew

Meaning: the Lord is my strength

V

Vail

Alternative uses: Vale, Vayl

Origin: British

Meaning: valley

Valentin

Alternative uses: Valintin, Val, Valentine

Origin: Latin

Meaning: strong

Valerian

Alternative uses: Val

Origin: Latin

Meaning: strong, healthy

Vallen

Alternative uses: Val, Vallin

Origin: Latin

Meaning: strong, healthy

Vander

Alternative uses: Evander, Vandar, Vandar

Origin: Greek

Meaning: good man

Vane

Alternative uses: Vain

Origin: British

Meaning: banner

Van

Alternative uses: Vann

Origin: Danish

Meaning: of, or from

Varen

Alternative uses: Var, Varin, Varan

Origin: unknown

Meaning: unknown

Varrick

Alternative uses: Varik, Varrik, Varric

Origin: German

Meaning: leader who defends

Velin

Alternative uses: Vel, Velen, Velan

Origin: unknown

Meaning: unknown

Venezio

Alternative uses: Vene, Venecio

Origin: Italian

Meaning: from Venice

Vern

Alternative uses: Virn

Origin: French

Meaning: alder grove

Vester

Alternative uses: Vest, Vestir, Vestar

Origin: Latin

Meaning: wooded

Victor

Alternative uses: Vick, Vic, Viktor

Origin: Latin

Meaning: champion

Viggo

Alternative uses: Vigo

Origin: unknown

Meaning: unknown

Vincent

Alternative uses: Vin, Vinny, Vince, Vincint

Origin: Latin

Meaning: prevailing

Virgil

Alternative uses: Virg, Virgel, Vergel

Origin: Latin

Meaning: staff-bearer

Vital

Alternative uses: Vit, Vitale, Vitall

Origin: Latin

Meaning: life-giving

Vladimir

Alternative uses: Vlad, Vladamir

Origin: Slavic

Meaning: renowned prince

Von

Alternative uses: Vaughn, Vaun

Origin: Norse

Meaning: hope

W

Wade

Alternative uses: Waid, Wayde

Origin: Scandinavian

Meaning: able to go

Wagner

Alternative uses: Wag, Wagnar

Origin: British

Meaning: wagon-builder

Wakely

Alternative uses: Wakeley, Wake

Origin: British

Meaning: morning meadow

Walcott

Alternative uses: Wal, Wall, Walcot

Origin: British

Meaning: cottage by the wall

Walden

Alternative uses: Waldan, Wald

Origin: British

Meaning: wooded valley

Wallace

Alternative uses: Wallis, Wallas, Wall

Origin: French

Meaning: Welshman

Waller

Alternative uses: Wall, Wallar

Origin: German

Meaning: powerful one

Walsh

Alternative uses: none

Origin: British

Meaning: from Wales

Walter

Alternative uses: Walt, Waltar

Origin: German

Meaning: commander of the army

Ward

Alternative uses: none

Origin: British

Meaning: watchman

Warrick

Alternative uses: Warr, Warrack

Origin: German

Meaning: leader who defends

Wash

Alternative uses: none

Origin: Irish

Meaning: on the go, energetic

Way

Alternative uses: Waye

Origin: British

Meaning: land by the road

Wayne

Alternative uses: Wane, Wain

Origin: British

Meaning: wagon builder

Weaver

Alternative uses: Weave, Weav

Origin: British

Meaning: clothing weaver

Webster

Alternative uses: Web, Webb, Webbster

Origin: British

Meaning: weaver

Wesley

Alternative uses: Wes, Weslee

Origin: British

Meaning: western meadow

Weston

Alternative uses: West, Westin

Origin: British

Meaning: western town

Wheatley

Alternative uses: Wheat, Weat, Weatl

Origin: British

Meaning: wheat meadow

Whitacker

Alternative uses: Whit, Wit, Witaker

Origin: British

Meaning: white field

William

Alternative uses: Will, Bill, Billy, Willem

Origin: German

Meaning: protection

Winton

Alternative uses: Win, Wint, Winten, Wintin

Origin: British

Meaning: house of a friend

Wolfe

Alternative uses: Wolf, Woolf

Origin: German

Meaning: wolf

Wright

Alternative uses: Write, Right

Origin: British

Meaning: carpenter

Wyatt

Alternative uses: Wyat, Wy, Wiatt

Origin: British

Meaning: war strength

Wyeth

Alternative uses: Wyath, Wiath

Origin: British

Meaning: war strength

X

Xander

Alternative uses: Zander, Xan

Origin: Greek

Meaning: defender of man

Xanthus

Alternative uses: Zanth, Xanth, Zanthis

Origin: Greek

Meaning: golden-haired

Xavier

Alternative uses: Xav, Xaviar

Origin: Spanish

Meaning: bright, splendid

Xenos

Alternative uses: Xeno, Xen, Zenos

Origin: Greek

Meaning: hospitality

Y

Yachim

Alternative uses: Yakeem, Yakim

Origin: Hebrew

Meaning: established by God

Yago

Alternative uses: none

Origin: Welsh

Meaning: he who supplants

Yale

Alternative uses: Yael, Yayl

Origin: Welsh

Meaning: heights, upland

Yamal

Alternative uses: none

Origin: Sanskrit

Meaning: one of twins

Yance

Alternative uses: Yans, Yancey

Origin: Native American

Meaning: Englishman

Yannis

Alternative uses: Yann, Yanice

Origin: Hebrew

Meaning: God is gracious

Yardley

Alternative uses: Yar, Yard, Yardly

Origin: British

Meaning: fenced meadow

Yasir

Alternative uses: Yaseer

Origin: Arabic

Meaning: well to do

Yates

Alternative uses: Yate, Yeats

Origin: British

Meaning: the gates

Yen

Alternative uses: none

Origin: Vietnamese

Meaning: calm

Yitro

Alternative uses: none

Origin: Hebrew

Meaning: excellence

Yoel

Alternative uses: none

Origin: Hebrew

Meaning: the Lord is God

Yonas

Alternative uses: Yon, Yonis

Origin: Hebrew

Meaning: dove

Yorick

Alternative uses: Yor, Yorrick, Yorik

Origin: British

Meaning: farmer

York

Alternative uses: Yorke

Origin: British

Meaning: place of boars

Young

Alternative uses: Yung, Youn

Origin: British

Meaning: youth

Yuan

Alternative uses: none

Origin: Hebrew

Meaning: God is merciful

Yury

Alternative uses: Yuri, Yur

Origin: Russian

Meaning: the light of God

Yvo

Alternative uses: Ivo

Origin: French

Meaning: yew tree

Z

Zachary

Alternative uses: Zach, Zak, Zakary

Origin: Hebrew

Meaning: God remembers

Zachariah

Alternative uses: Zac, Zakaria, Ria

Origin: Hebrew

Meaning: God remembers

Zaid

Alternative uses: Zayd, Zade

Origin: Arabic

Meaning: master

Zander

Alternative uses: Zan, Xander

Origin: Slavic

Meaning: defender of men

Zane

Alternative uses: Zayn, Zain

Origin: Hebrew

Meaning: God is gracious

Zay

Alternative uses: Zai

Origin: unknown

Meaning: unknown

Zebediah

Alternative uses: Zeb, Zebadia, Zebedia

Origin: Hebrew

Meaning: gift of God

Zeke

Alternative uses: Zeek, Zek

Origin: British

Meaning: God remembers

Zeno

Alternative uses: Zino, Zeen, Zin

Origin: Greek

Meaning: gift of Zeus

Zeph

Alternative uses: Zef, Seph, Sef

Origin: Hebrew

Meaning: hidden by God

Zeus

Alternative uses: Zuse

Origin: Greek

Meaning: living

Zer

Alternative uses: Zir, Zur

Origin: Hebrew

Meaning: wreath

Zev

Alternative uses: none

Origin: Hebrew

Meaning: given by God

Zion

Alternative uses: Zyon, Zi, Zy

Origin: Hebrew

Meaning: highest point

Zon

Alternative uses: none

Origin: Yiddish

Meaning: little son

Zuriel

Alternative uses: Zureyl, Zuri

Origin: Hebrew

Meaning: God is my rock

Girl Names

The names in this glossary have been predominantly used for girls throughout their use in history, though there is no rule that the same names can't be given to boys (for a collection of androgynous names, see the corresponding list). They are listed alphabetically and offer multiple spellings and possible shortenings and nicknames.

A

Aaliyah
Alternative uses: Liyah, Aliya
Origin: Hebrew
Meaning: rising

Abigail
Alternative uses: Abby, Abygail, Abigale
Origin: Hebrew
Meaning: wisdom

Ada
Alternative uses: Adah, Aida, Adele
Origin: German
Meaning: noble

Adaline
Alternative uses: Adalyn, Adalene
Origin: German
Meaning: noble race

Adelaide
Alternative uses: Addy, Adilaide, Adi
Origin: German
Meaning: noble race

Addison
Alternative uses: Addi, Adison
Origin: British
Meaning: son of Adam

Aisha
Alternative uses: Aysha, Aish, Aysh
Origin: Arabic
Meaning: alive

Aleah
Alternative uses: Alea, Alia, Aleea
Origin: Hebrew
Meaning: rising

Alexa
Alternative uses: Alexis, Lexi, Lexie
Origin: Greek
Meaning: defender of man

Alexandria
Alternative uses: Alessandra, Alexandra
Origin: Greek
Meaning: defender of man

Alicia
Alternative uses: Alice, Alisha
Origin: German
Meaning: exalted

Alana
Alternative uses: Alannah, Alanna
Origin: Latin
Meaning: precious

Alina
Alternative uses: Alin, Alinna, Alinea
Origin: French
Meaning: noble

Allison

Alternative uses: Alison, Ally, Alli

Origin: German

Meaning: noble

Alyssa

Alternative uses: Alisa, Alysa, Alys

Origin: Greek

Meaning: rational

Amara

Alternative uses: none

Origin: Latin

Meaning: everlasting

Amber

Alternative uses: Ambyr, Ambe

Origin: Sanskrit

Meaning: the sky

Amelia

Alternative uses: Amilia

Origin: Latin

Meaning: industrious

Amy

Alternative uses: Aimee, Aime

Origin: Latin

Meaning: beloved

Andrea

Alternative uses: Andi, Andy, Andraya

Origin: Greek

Meaning: lively

Angela

Alternative uses: Angie, Angelica, Angelina

Origin: Latin

Meaning: messenger

Anna

Alternative uses: Ana

Origin: Hebrew

Meaning: God has favored me

Annabelle

Alternative uses: Anabell, Anabel

Origin: Hebrew

Meaning: favored grace

Annaliese

Alternative uses: Anaalisa, Annalise

Origin: Latin

Meaning: graced with God's bounty

Annika

Alternative uses: Anika, Anica

Origin: Hebrew

Meaning: sweet-faced

April

Alternative uses: Apryl

Origin: Latin

Meaning: to open

Arely

Alternative uses: Aurelia, Aurelie, Arel

Origin: Latin

Meaning: golden

Ariadne

Alternative uses: none

Origin: Greek

Meaning: most holy

Ariana

Alternative uses: Ari, Aryana

Origin: Welsh

Meaning: silver

Ariel

Alternative uses: Arielle, Erielle

Origin: Hebrew

Meaning: lion of God

Ashley

Alternative uses: Ashleigh

Origin: British

Meaning: ash meadow

Ashton

Alternative uses: Ashten, Ash

Origin: British

Meaning: ash tree town

Asia

Alternative uses: Aza

Origin: Greek

Meaning: sunrise

Astrid

Alternative uses: Astryd

Origin: Norse

Meaning: fair, beautiful goddess

Athena

Alternative uses: none

Origin: Greek

Meaning: wise

Ava

Alternative uses: Avah

Origin: Hebrew

Meaning: life

Avery

Alternative uses: Avary

Origin: British

Meaning: elf counsel

Avianna

Alternative uses: Avi, Aviana

Origin: British

Meaning: life

Aubrey

Alternative uses: Aubree, Aubri

Origin: German

Meaning: power

Audrey

Alternative uses: Audri, Adrey

Origin: British

Meaning: noble strength

Aurora

Alternative uses: none

Origin: Latin

Meaning: dawn

B

Baylie

Alternative uses: Baylee, Bailee

Origin: British

Meaning: bailiff

Barbara

Alternative uses: Barb, Barbie

Origin: Latin

Meaning: foreign woman

Beatrice

Alternative uses: Bea, Beatrix, Tricia

Origin: Latin

Meaning: blessed

Bella

Alternative uses: Belle, Bela

Origin: Latin

Meaning: beautiful

Bernadette

Alternative uses: Berna, Bernadet

Origin: German

Meaning: brave bear

Bernice

Alternative uses: Berenice

Origin: Greek

Meaning: victory bringer

Bethany

Alternative uses: Beth, Bethani, Betha

Origin: Hebrew

Meaning: house of figs

Blanca

Alternative uses: Blanc, Blanka

Origin: Italian

Meaning: white and pure

Bianca

Alternative uses: none

Origin: Italian

Meaning: white and pure

Bonnie

Alternative uses: Bonny, Bon

Origin: Scottish

Meaning: pretty

Braelyn

Alternative uses: Brae

Origin: unknown

Meaning: unknown

Brandy

Alternative uses: Brandee

Origin: Italian

Meaning: sword

Brenna

Alternative uses: Brynna, Brynn

Origin: Gaelic

Meaning: raven-haired

Bria

Alternative uses: Bri, Brie

Origin: Irish

Meaning: noble

Brisa

Alternative uses: Breesa, Bris

Origin: Latin

Meaning: from Briseis in Homer's "Iliad"

Briana

Alternative uses: none

Origin: Irish

Meaning: exalted

Bridget

Alternative uses: none

Origin: Gaelic

Meaning: exalted one

Britney

Alternative uses: Brittany, Britt, Briton

Origin: Latin

Meaning: from Britain

Brooklyn

Alternative uses: none

Origin: German

Meaning: water

C

Callie

Alternative uses: Cali, Calista

Origin: Greek

Meaning: beautiful

Caitlyn

Alternative uses: Caitlin, Cait

Origin: Greek

Meaning: pure

Camila

Alternative uses: Camilla, Mila

Origin: Latin

Meaning: helper to the priest

Camryn

Alternative uses: Cameron, Cam

Origin: Scottish

Meaning: crooked nose

Carly

Alternative uses: Carli

Origin: Latin

Meaning: free man

Carolina

Alternative uses: Carolin, Caroline

Origin: German

Meaning: free man

Cassandra

Alternative uses: Cassy, Cassia, Cassie

Origin: Greek

Meaning: warrior

Catherine

Alternative uses: Katherine, Kathy, Kate

Origin: Greek

Meaning: pure

Catalina

Alternative uses: Cate

Origin: Greek

Meaning: pure

Celine

Alternative uses: Celina

Origin: Latin

Meaning: heaven

Celeste

Alternative uses: none

Origin: Latin

Meaning: heavenly

Charlotte

Alternative uses: Char, Charley

Origin: German

Meaning: free

Chloe

Alternative uses: Kloe

Origin: Greek

Meaning: green shoot

Christina

Alternative uses: Chris, Christine

Origin: Latin

Meaning: follower of Christ

Clara

Alternative uses: Claire, Claer

Origin: Latin

Meaning: bright

Clarissa

Alternative uses: Clarice

Origin: Latin

Meaning: bright

Clementine

Alternative uses: none

Origin: Latin

Meaning: merciful

Colette

Alternative uses: Collete, Collette

Origin: French

Meaning: people of victory

Crystal

Alternative uses: Cristal, Chrystal

Origin: Greek

Meaning: ice

Cynthia

Alternative uses: Cynth, Cindy

Origin: Greek

Meaning: light

D

Dahlia

Alternative uses: none

Origin: Swedish

Meaning: valley

Daisy

Alternative uses: Daizy

Origin: British

Meaning: day's eye

Damaris

Alternative uses: none

Origin: Latin

Meaning: gentle

Dana

Alternative uses: none

Origin: British

Meaning: from Denmark

Danica

Alternative uses: Danyka, Danika

Origin: Slavic

Meaning: morning star

Danielle

Alternative uses: Dani, Dany, Danyel

Origin: Hebrew

Meaning: God is my judge

Daphne

Alternative uses: Daph, Dafne

Origin: Greek

Meaning: laurel tree

Darcy

Alternative uses: Darci

Origin: Irish

Meaning: dark

Daria

Alternative uses: Darya

Origin: Persian

Meaning: maintains possessions well

Davina

Alternative uses: Davin, Devina

Origin: Scottish

Meaning: beloved

Dawn

Alternative uses: none

Origin: British

Meaning: daybreak

Deborah

Alternative uses: Deb, Debra

Origin: Hebrew

Meaning: bee

Demi

Alternative uses: none

Origin: French

Meaning: half

Denise

Alternative uses: Denice

Origin: French

Meaning: follows Dionysus, god of mirth

Devon

Alternative uses: Devin, Dev

Origin: British

Meaning: for Devon, a county in England

Destiny

Alternative uses: Destyn, Destyny

Origin: French

Meaning: fate

Diana

Alternative uses: Diane, Dyan

Origin: Latin

Meaning: divine

Dora

Alternative uses: none

Origin: Greek

Meaning: gift

Dove

Alternative uses: none

Origin: unknown

Meaning: a bird symbolizing peace

E

Edith

Alternative uses: Edie, Edi

Origin: British

Meaning: pursues wealth

Eleanor

Alternative uses: Elinor, Elanore

Origin: Greek

Meaning: shining light

Elizabeth

Alternative uses: Eliza, Lizzy, Liz

Origin: Hebrew

Meaning: God's promise

Ella

Alternative uses: Ela

Origin: German

Meaning: foreign

Eloise

Alternative uses: Heloise

Origin: German

Meaning: famous warrior

Elsa

Alternative uses: Ilsa

Origin: Hebrew

Meaning: God's promise

Emily

Alternative uses: Emilee, Emile

Origin: Latin

Meaning: rival

Emma

Alternative uses: Ema, Emmy

Origin: German

Meaning: entire

Erica

Alternative uses: Erika, Arica

Origin: Norse

Meaning: ruler

Esperanza

Alternative uses: Espi

Origin: Spanish

Meaning: hope

Etta

Alternative uses: none

Origin: Italian

Meaning: feminine

Evangeline

Alternative uses: Ev, Evangelina

Origin: Greek

Meaning: good news

Evelyn

Alternative uses: Ev, Evie, Evelinn

Origin: French

Meaning: life

F

Faith

Alternative uses: none

Origin: British

Meaning: loyalty

Fantine

Alternative uses: Fanny

Origin: Latin

Meaning: from France

Farah

Alternative uses: Fara, Farrah

Origin: British

Meaning: good-looking

Fatima

Alternative uses: Fati

Origin: Arabic

Meaning: captivating

Fawn

Alternative uses: none

Origin: French

Meaning: young deer

Felicity

Alternative uses: Felicia

Origin: Latin

Meaning: happy

Fern

Alternative uses: none

Origin: British

Meaning: fern

Fiona

Alternative uses: none

Origin: Irish

Meaning: fair

Flora

Alternative uses: none

Origin: Latin

Meaning: flower

Fortuna

Alternative uses: Fortune

Origin: Latin

Meaning: good fate

Francesca

Alternative uses: Cesca

Origin: Latin

Meaning: from France

Freya

Alternative uses: Freja, Freia

Origin: Scandinavian

Meaning: noble lady

G

Gabrielle

Alternative uses: Gabi, Gaby, Gabriella

Origin: Hebrew

Meaning: heroine of God

Gemma

Alternative uses: Gema, Jemma

Origin: Latin

Meaning: jewel

Genevieve

Alternative uses: Gen, Genivive

Origin: French

Meaning: of the race of women

Georgia

Alternative uses: Jorja, Georja

Origin: Latin

Meaning: farmer

Gianna

Alternative uses: Gian, Gia

Origin: Italian

Meaning: God is gracious

Gina

Alternative uses: none

Origin: Greek

Meaning: noble

Ginny

Alternative uses: Gin

Origin: Latin

Meaning: virgin

Giselle

Alternative uses: Gis, Gizelle

Origin: German

Meaning: pledge

Golda

Alternative uses: Goldie, Goldy

Origin: British

Meaning: precious, gold

Grace

Alternative uses: Gracie

Origin: Latin

Meaning: blessing

Grier

Alternative uses: Greer

Origin: Scottish

Meaning: watchful

Greta

Alternative uses: none

Origin: German

Meaning: pearl

Gwen

Alternative uses: Gwyn, Gwennie

Origin: Welsh

Meaning: blessed

Gwyneth

Alternative uses: none

Origin: Welsh

Meaning: happiness

H

Hannah

Alternative uses: Hanna

Origin: Hebrew

Meaning: favored by God

Harlie

Alternative uses: Harley, Harlee

Origin: British

Meaning: hare meadow

Harper

Alternative uses: none

Origin: British

Meaning: minstrel

Harriet

Alternative uses: Hattie

Origin: German

Meaning: home ruler

Hayley

Alternative uses: Haley, Haleigh

Origin: Norse

Meaning: hero

Heather

Alternative uses: none

Origin: British

Meaning: flowering plant

Heaven

Alternative uses: Haven

Origin: unknown

Meaning: sky

Heidi

Alternative uses: Hydi, Hydie

Origin: German

Meaning: nobility

Heily

Alternative uses: Hylee, Hyly

Origin: unknown

Meaning: unknown

Helen

Alternative uses: Helene

Origin: Greek

Meaning: shining light

Holly

Alternative uses: Hollee, Holli

Origin: British

Meaning: holly tree

I

Ida

Alternative uses: Eida

Origin: Greek

Meaning: hardworking

Iliana

Alternative uses: none

Origin: Greek

Meaning: from Troy, a strong city

Ilse

Alternative uses: Ilsa, Elsa

Origin: German

Meaning: oath of God

Imogen

Alternative uses: Imogene

Origin: Irish

Meaning: maiden

Ingrid

Alternative uses: Ingred

Origin: Scandinavian

Meaning: beauty of a goddess

Iona

Alternative uses: none

Origin: Greek

Meaning: blessed

Irene

Alternative uses: Irina

Origin: Greek

Meaning: peace

Iris

Alternative uses: none

Origin: Greek

Meaning: rainbow

Isabelle

Alternative uses: Isabella, Isa, Izzy

Origin: Hebrew

Meaning: God's promise

Ishani

Alternative uses: none

Origin: Hindi

Meaning: desire

Ivy

Alternative uses: Ivee

Origin: British

Meaning: climbing plant

J

Jacie

Alternative uses: Jacee

Origin: American

Meaning: unknown

Jacqueline

Alternative uses: Jakelynn, Jackie

Origin: French

Meaning: he who supplants

Jaden

Alternative uses: Jade, Jadin, Jayden

Origin: American

Meaning: unknown

Jamie

Alternative uses: Jami

Origin: Hebrew

Meaning: he who supplants

Janaye

Alternative uses: Janay

Origin: Hebrew

Meaning: God is gracious

Jane

Alternative uses: Janie, Janice

Origin: Hebrew

Meaning: God is gracious

Janelle

Alternative uses: Janel

Origin: American

Meaning: God is gracious

January

Alternative uses: Jan

Origin: unknown

Meaning: for Janus, god of beginnings

Jasmine

Alternative uses: Jas, Jazzy

Origin: Persian

Meaning: perfumed flower

Jaya

Alternative uses: Jay, Jaia

Origin: Hindi

Meaning: victorious

Jean

Alternative uses: Jeannie

Origin: Hebrew

Meaning: God is gracious

Jenna

Alternative uses: Jena

Origin: Arabic

Meaning: heaven

Jennifer

Alternative uses: Jen, Jenny, Jenifer

Origin: Welsh

Meaning: fair one

Jessica

Alternative uses: Jess, Jessi, Jesse

Origin: Hebrew

Meaning: God sees

Jewel

Alternative uses: none

Origin: French

Meaning: delight

Jillian

Alternative uses: Jill, Gillian

Origin: Latin

Meaning: youthful

Joan

Alternative uses: Jone

Origin: Hebrew

Meaning: God is gracious

Joanna

Alternative uses: Jo, Joann, Johanna

Origin: French

Meaning: God is gracious

Jocelyn

Alternative uses: Joselyn

Origin: German

Meaning: of the German tribe

Jolene

Alternative uses: none

Origin: American

Meaning: God will increase

Joni

Alternative uses: none

Origin: Hebrew

Meaning: God is gracious

Jordan

Alternative uses: Jordi

Origin: Hebrew

Meaning: down-flowing

Josephine

Alternative uses: Jo, Josefina

Origin: Hebrew

Meaning: God increases

Josie

Alternative uses: Josi, Josee

Origin: British

Meaning: God increases

Joy

Alternative uses: none

Origin: Latin

Meaning: joy

Judy

Alternative uses: none

Origin: Hebrew

Meaning: praised

Julie

Alternative uses: Julia, Juliet, Jules

Origin: French

Meaning: youthful

June

Alternative uses: Juno

Origin: Latin

Meaning: young

Justine

Alternative uses: Justyne, Just

Origin: Latin

Meaning: upright

K

Kaia

Alternative uses: Kaya

Origin: Hawaiian

Meaning: the sea

Kaitlyn

Alternative uses: Kait, Katelyn

Origin: Greek

Meaning: pure

Kara

Alternative uses: Cara

Origin: Latin

Meaning: beloved

Karla

Alternative uses: Carla

Origin: Greek

Meaning: strength

Katherine

Alternative uses: Kat, Kate, Katarina

Origin: Greek

Meaning: pure

Kaylee

Alternative uses: Kaylie, Kailey, Kayla

Origin: Gaelic

Meaning: slender

Keira

Alternative uses: Kiera

Origin: Irish

Meaning: dark

Kelly

Alternative uses: Kell, Kelli

Origin: Irish

Meaning: descendant of Ceallach

Kelsey

Alternative uses: Kelsi, Kels

Origin: British

Meaning: victorious ship

Kendall

Alternative uses: Kendell

Origin: British

Meaning: river valley

Kendra

Alternative uses: none

Origin: Welsh

Meaning: greatest champion

Kimberly

Alternative uses: Kim, Kimmer

Origin: British

Meaning: royal forest

Kira

Alternative uses: Ciara

Origin: Greek

Meaning: lord

Kora

Alternative uses: Cora

Origin: Greek

Meaning: maiden

Kylie

Alternative uses: none

Origin: Irish

Meaning: narrow, straight

L

Lacy

Alternative uses: Laci, Lacey

Origin: French

Meaning: a place in France

Lana

Alternative uses: none

Origin: Irish

Meaning: child

Lara

Alternative uses: Lares

Origin: Latin

Meaning: protection

Laura

Alternative uses: Lora, Laurie

Origin: Latin

Meaning: laurel plant

Lauren

Alternative uses: none
Origin: Latin
Meaning: laurel plant

Layla
Alternative uses: Laila, Laela
Origin: Arabic
Meaning: night beauty

Leah
Alternative uses: Lea, Leia
Origin: Hebrew
Meaning: delicate

Leanne
Alternative uses: Leanna, Liann
Origin: British
Meaning: to twine around

Leigh
Alternative uses: Lee
Origin: Hebrew
Meaning: delicate

Lena
Alternative uses: Lina, Leena
Origin: unknown
Meaning: torch

Leonora
Alternative uses: Lenore, Leonore
Origin: Greek
Meaning: light

Leticia
Alternative uses: Lettie
Origin: Latin
Meaning: joy

Libby
Alternative uses: none

Origin: Hebrew
Meaning: God's promise

Liesel
Alternative uses: Liesl, Leisel
Origin:
Meaning:

Lillian
Alternative uses: Lily
Origin: Latin
Meaning: lily

Lindsey
Alternative uses: Lindsay, Lindy
Origin: British
Meaning: island of linden trees

Loni
Alternative uses: none
Origin: Latin
Meaning: lion

Lorelai
Alternative uses: none
Origin: unknown
Meaning: unknown

Louise
Alternative uses: Lou, Louisa
Origin: German
Meaning: famous warrior

Lucia
Alternative uses: Lusiya, Luz, Lucy
Origin: Italian
Meaning: light

Lydia
Alternative uses: Liddy
Origin: Greek

Meaning: from Lydia, a region in Asia

Lyla

Alternative uses: Lila

Origin: British

Meaning: island beauty

M

Macy

Alternative uses: Maci, Macee

Origin: French

Meaning: weapon

Mackenzie

Alternative uses: Kenzie

Origin: Scottish

Meaning: fire-born

Madeline

Alternative uses: Madeleine, Madilynn

Origin: Hebrew

Meaning: great

Madison

Alternative uses: Maddie, Madysen

Origin: British

Meaning: son of a mighty warrior

Maisie

Alternative uses: Mayzee

Origin: Scottish

Meaning: pearl

Margaret

Alternative uses: Maggie, Megan, Margot

Origin: Greek

Meaning: pearl

Mariah

Alternative uses: Maria, Moriah

Origin: Latin

Meaning: God is my teacher

Marina

Alternative uses: Mina

Origin: Latin

Meaning: by the sea

Marissa

Alternative uses: none

Origin: Latin

Meaning: by the sea

Marley

Alternative uses: Marlee

Origin: German

Meaning: marshy meadow

Marlow

Alternative uses: Marlo

Origin: British

Meaning: driftwood

Mary

Alternative uses: Marie, Maria, Mari

Origin: Latin

Meaning: star of the sea

May

Alternative uses: Mae

Origin: Sanskrit

Meaning: the fifth month

Melanie

Alternative uses: Mel

Origin: Greek

Meaning: dark-skinned

Melissa

Alternative uses: Missy

Origin: Greek

Meaning: bee or honey

Melody

Alternative uses: Mel, Melodee

Origin: Greek

Meaning: music

Mercedes

Alternative uses: Cerdes, Marcy

Origin: Spanish

Meaning: mercies

Mia

Alternative uses: Mya

Origin: Scandinavian

Meaning: beloved

Michaela

Alternative uses: Mica, Michelle

Origin: Hebrew

Meaning: who is like God

Mila

Alternative uses: none

Origin: Spanish

Meaning: miraculous

Miranda

Alternative uses: none

Origin: Latin

Meaning: admiration

Miriam

Alternative uses: none

Origin: Hebrew

Meaning: wished-for child

Molly

Alternative uses: Moll

Origin: Irish

Meaning: star of the sea

N

Nadia

Alternative uses: Nadya

Origin: Russian

Meaning: hope

Naomi

Alternative uses: Noemie

Origin: Hebrew

Meaning: pleasant

Natalie

Alternative uses: Nat, Nataly, Natasha

Origin: Latin

Meaning: birthday

Nerissa

Alternative uses: none

Origin: Italian

Meaning: dark-haired

Niamh

Alternative uses: Neev, Neeve

Origin: Irish

Meaning: radiant beauty

Nicole

Alternative uses: Nikki, Nikole, Nichole

Origin: Greek

Meaning: people of victory

Nina

Alternative uses: none

Origin: Spanish

Meaning: little girl

Noel

Alternative uses: Noelle

Origin: French

Meaning: Christmas

Nora

Alternative uses: Norah
Origin: Latin
Meaning: honor

Nova
Alternative uses: none
Origin: Latin
Meaning: new

O

Octavia
Alternative uses: Octave
Origin: Latin
Meaning: eighth

Olivia
Alternative uses: Oliva, Liv, Livia
Origin: Latin
Meaning: olive tree

Olwyn
Alternative uses: Olwin
Origin: Welsh
Meaning: pale footprint

Opal
Alternative uses: none
Origin: Sanskrit
Meaning: jewel

P

Paige
Alternative uses: Page
Origin: British
Meaning: young servant

Pamela
Alternative uses: Pam, Pammy
Origin: Greek
Meaning: sweetness

Paola
Alternative uses: Paula
Origin: Latin
Meaning: small

Paris
Alternative uses: none
Origin: Greek
Meaning: a Trojan prince

Parker
Alternative uses: none
Origin: British
Meaning: park keeper

Patrice
Alternative uses: Patricia, Tricia
Origin: Latin
Meaning: noble

Pearl
Alternative uses: Perla
Origin: Latin
Meaning: pearl, precious

Penelope
Alternative uses: Penny
Origin: Greek
Meaning: weaver

Petra
Alternative uses: none
Origin: Greek
Meaning: rock

Peyton
Alternative uses: Payton, Paytin
Origin: Irish
Meaning: unknown

Phedra

Alternative uses: Fedra, Phe

Origin: Greek

Meaning: bright

Philippa

Alternative uses: Pippa

Origin: Greek

Meaning: lover of horses

Phoebe

Alternative uses: none

Origin: Greek

Meaning: bright

Piper

Alternative uses: none

Origin: British

Meaning: pipe player

Portia

Alternative uses: Porsha

Origin: Latin

Meaning: offering

Q

Quinn

Alternative uses: Kwyn, Quenn

Origin: Irish

Meaning: counselor

Quintessa

Alternative uses: none

Origin: Latin

Meaning: fifth

Quita

Alternative uses: Kita

Origin: unknown

Meaning: light

R

Rachel

Alternative uses: Raechel, Rashelle, Rae

Origin: Hebrew

Meaning: female sheep

Raina

Alternative uses: Reina, Raena, Rainey

Origin: Irish

Meaning: queen

Ramona

Alternative uses: Mona

Origin: Spanish

Meaning: protecting hands

Raven

Alternative uses: Ravena, Ravenna

Origin: British

Meaning: black bird

Rebecca

Alternative uses: Rebekah. Becca

Origin: Hebrew

Meaning: to bind

Regina

Alternative uses: none

Origin: Latin

Meaning: queen

Renee

Alternative uses: Renae

Origin: French

Meaning: reborn

Rhianna

Alternative uses: Rianna, Rhianne

Origin: Welsh

Meaning: great queen

Rhoda

Alternative uses: none

Origin: Latin

Meaning: rose

Robin

Alternative uses: Robyn

Origin: German

Meaning: bright fame

Rose

Alternative uses: Rosa, Rosie

Origin: Latin

Meaning: rose

Rosamund

Alternative uses: Rosamond

Origin: German

Meaning: protector of horses

Rosalind

Alternative uses: none

Origin: German

Meaning: gentle horse

Roxanne

Alternative uses: Roxy, Roxi

Origin: Persian

Meaning: dawn

Ruby

Alternative uses: Rubie, Rube

Origin: British

Meaning: gem

Ruth

Alternative uses: Ruthie

Origin: Hebrew

Meaning: friend

Ryann

Alternative uses: Riann

Origin: Irish

Meaning: king

Rylie

Alternative uses: Wrylie

Origin: Irish

Meaning: rye clearing

S

Sabrina

Alternative uses: Sabrine

Origin: Celtic

Meaning: from the river

Sadie

Alternative uses: Saydee

Origin: Hebrew

Meaning: princess

Saida

Alternative uses: Sayda

Origin: Arabic

Meaning: fortunate

Samantha

Alternative uses: Sam, Sammy

Origin: Hebrew

Meaning: God heard

Sandra

Alternative uses: Sandy

Origin: Italian

Meaning: man's defender

Sarah

Alternative uses: Sara, Sarai

Origin: Hebrew

Meaning: princess

Sasha

Alternative uses: none

Origin: Russian

Meaning: man's defender

Saoirse

Alternative uses: Shersha

Origin: Irish

Meaning: freedom

Saskia

Alternative uses: Saskya

Origin: Slavic

Meaning: from Saxony

Savannah

Alternative uses: Sav, Savanna

Origin: Spanish

Meaning: treeless

Scarlett

Alternative uses: Scarlet

Origin: French

Meaning: red

Scout

Alternative uses: none

Origin: French

Meaning: listener

Selene

Alternative uses: Selena

Origin: Greek

Meaning: the moon

Serena

Alternative uses: Serene

Origin: Latin

Meaning: calm

Shannon

Alternative uses: none

Origin: Gaelic

Meaning: ancient

Sharon

Alternative uses: Shari, Sharen

Origin: Hebrew

Meaning: fertile plain

Shawna

Alternative uses: Shawn, Shauna

Origin: Irish

Meaning: God is gracious

Shea

Alternative uses: Shay

Origin: Gaelic

Meaning: admirable

Sheila

Alternative uses: none

Origin: Latin

Meaning: heavenly

Shelby

Alternative uses: none

Origin: Norse

Meaning: willow

Sidney

Alternative uses: Sydney, Syd

Origin: British

Meaning: wide meadow

Sierra

Alternative uses: Cierra

Origin: Spanish

Meaning: mountains

Simone

Alternative uses: Symone

Origin: Hebrew

Meaning: hearing

Siobhan

Alternative uses: Shivon

Origin: Irish

Meaning: God is gracious

Sophia

Alternative uses: Sophie, Sofia, Sofi

Origin: Greek

Meaning: wisdom

Stacey

Alternative uses: Staci, Stacee

Origin: Greek

Meaning: resurrection

Starla

Alternative uses: none

Origin: Persian

Meaning: star

Stephanie

Alternative uses: Steph, Steff, Stefani

Origin: Greek

Meaning: crown

Stormy

Alternative uses: Stormi

Origin: British

Meaning: stormy

Summer

Alternative uses: none

Origin: British

Meaning: summer

Susanna

Alternative uses: Susan, Susannah, Susie

Origin: Hebrew

Meaning: lily

T

Tabitha

Alternative uses: Tabi

Origin: Aramaic

Meaning: gazelle

Taira

Alternative uses: Tara

Origin: Sanskrit

Meaning: star

Talise

Alternative uses: Tali, Taleese

Origin: Native American

Meaning: lovely water

Tamara

Alternative uses: Tammy, Tamra

Origin: Hebrew

Meaning: date palm

Tana

Alternative uses: none

Origin: Russian

Meaning: fire goddess

Taryn

Alternative uses: none

Origin: British

Meaning: thunder

Tatiana

Alternative uses: Tat, Tati

Origin: Russian

Meaning: royalty

Tatum

Alternative uses: none

Origin: British

Meaning: unknown

Tawny

Alternative uses: Tawni
Origin: Irish
Meaning: golden

Tawnya
Alternative uses: Tonya
Origin: Russian
Meaning: fire goddess

Teresa
Alternative uses: Terri, Theresa
Origin: Greek
Meaning: late summer

Tessa
Alternative uses: Tess
Origin: Greek
Meaning: late summer

Thandie
Alternative uses: Tandy, Tandi
Origin: Norse
Meaning: warrior

Thea
Alternative uses: none
Origin: Greek
Meaning: goddess

Tiana
Alternative uses: none
Origin: Russian
Meaning: princess

Tiffany
Alternative uses: Tifani, Tiff
Origin: Greek
Meaning: revelation of God

Tilly
Alternative uses: none

Origin: German
Meaning: mighty in battle

Tori
Alternative uses: Tory
Origin: Japanese
Meaning: bird

Tracy
Alternative uses: Tracey, Traci
Origin: Latin
Meaning: warlike

Trinity
Alternative uses: Trin
Origin: Latin
Meaning: triad

U

Ultima
Alternative uses: none
Origin: Latin
Meaning: farthest point

Unity
Alternative uses: none
Origin: British
Meaning: oneness

Ursula
Alternative uses: Ursa
Origin: Scandinavian
Meaning: little bear

V

Valerie
Alternative uses: Val
Origin: Latin
Meaning: strong

Valentine

Alternative uses: none

Origin: Latin

Meaning: strong

Vanessa

Alternative uses: Van, Nessa

Origin: Greek

Meaning: butterfly

Vega

Alternative uses: none

Origin: Arabic

Meaning: star

Veronica

Alternative uses: none

Origin: Latin

Meaning: true image

Victoria

Alternative uses: Vicki, Viki

Origin: Latin

Meaning: victory

Violet

Alternative uses: Vi, Vyolet

Origin: Latin

Meaning: royal

Virginia

Alternative uses: Ginny, Gin

Origin: Latin

Meaning: maiden

Vivian

Alternative uses: Viv

Origin: Latin

Meaning: lively

W

Wendy

Alternative uses: Wendi

Origin: British

Meaning: friend

Whitney

Alternative uses: Witney, Whit

Origin: British

Meaning: White Island

Willa

Alternative uses: none

Origin: German

Meaning: protection

Willow

Alternative uses: none

Origin: British

Meaning: willow bay

Winifred

Alternative uses: Winnie, Winn

Origin: Welsh

Meaning: joy and peace

Wren

Alternative uses: Ren, Wryn

Origin: British

Meaning: songbird

Wynona

Alternative uses: Wyn, Winona

Origin: Native American

Meaning: first-born daughter

X

Xenia

Alternative uses: Kesenya

Origin: Greek

Meaning: guest

Y

Yasmin

Alternative uses: Yas

Origin: Persian

Meaning: jasmine flower

Ynes

Alternative uses: Ynez

Origin: Spanish

Meaning: pure

Yolanda

Alternative uses: none

Origin: Spanish

Meaning: violet flower

Yvette

Alternative uses: none

Origin: French

Meaning:

Z

Zahira

Alternative uses: none

Origin: Arabic

Meaning: brilliant

Zanetta

Alternative uses: none

Origin: Spanish

Meaning: God's gift

Zara

Alternative uses: none

Origin: Arabic

Meaning: radiance

Zetta

Alternative uses: none

Origin: Hebrew

Meaning: olive

Zoe

Alternative uses: Zoey

Origin: Greek

Meaning: life

Zora

Alternative uses: none

Origin: Slavic

Meaning: dawn

Zuri

Alternative uses: none

Origin: Swahili

Meaning: beautiful

If you enjoyed this book, can you please
leave a review for it on Amazon?

Made in the USA
Middletown, DE
22 February 2019